THE HOLOCAUST

Selected Documents in Eighteen Volumes

John Mendelsohn
EDITOR

Donald S. Detwiler
ADVISORY EDITOR

A GARLAND SERIES

CONTENTS OF THE SERIES

THE HOLOCAUST

16. Rescue to the Switzerland
The Musy and Saly Mayer Affairs

Introduction by
Sybil Milton

GARLAND PUBLISHING, INC.
NEW YORK · LONDON
1982

These documents have been reproduced from copies in
the National Archives. Dr. Mendelsohn's work was carried out entirely on his own time and without endorse-
ment or official participation by the National Archives as
an agency.

Library of Congress Cataloging in Publication Data
Main entry under title:

Rescue to Switzerland.

(The Holocaust ; 16)
1. World War, 1939–1945—Jews—Rescue—Switzerland—Sources.
2. Refugees, Jewish—Switzerland—Sources.
3. Jews—Switzerland—Politics and government—Sources.
4. Mayer, Saly, 1882–1950.   5. Switzerland—
Ethnic relations—Sources. I. Milton, Sybil. II. Series.
D810.J4H655   vol. 16   940.53′15′03924s   81-80324
[DS135.S9]   [940.53′15′039240494]   AACR2
ISBN 0-8240-4890-3

Design by Jonathan Billing

The volumes in this series have been printed on acid-free,
250-year-life paper.

Printed in the United States of America

ACKNOWLEDGMENTS

I owe a debt of gratitude to many people who aided me during various stages of preparing these eighteen volumes. Of these I would like to mention by name a few without whose generous efforts this publication would have been impossible. I would like to thank Donald B. Schewe of the Franklin D. Roosevelt Library in Hyde Park, New York, for his speedy and effective help. Sally Marcks and Richard Gould of the Diplomatic Branch of the National Archives in Washington, D.C., extended help beyond their normal archival duties, as did Timothy Mulligan and George Wagner from the Modern Military Branch. Edward J. McCarter in the Still Picture Branch helped a great deal. I would also like to thank my wife, Tish, for letting me spend my evenings during the past few years with these volumes rather than with her and our children, Michael and Lisa.

J. M.

INTRODUCTION

All schemes to effect the mass rescue of European Jews between 1939 and 1944 were unequivocal fiascos. Political expediency, indifference, and open hostility faced Jewish refugees in both allied and neutral nations. Immediately after the outbreak of war in 1939 fantastic and often desperate resettlement schemes to improbable locations—Ethiopia, Angola, British Guyana—multiplied; they foundered on their obvious impracticality. Limited safe havens for small numbers of Jewish and other civilian refugees were found in Shanghai, Palestine, Portugal, Spain, Turkey, Sweden, and Switzerland. After 1941 restrictive American immigration policies, British hostility to Jewish resettlement in Palestine, and international apathy doomed most Jews to death in the ghettos and concentration camps of occupied Europe. By early 1943 rumors and eyewitness accounts of mass murder reached neutral and allied nations, but military considerations and widespread anti-Semitism resulted in the calculated inaction of the Anglo-American Bermuda conference on refugees, which met in April 1943 while the Nazis destroyed the Warsaw ghetto.

The policy of "rescue through victory" slowly changed in 1944. The military situation had radically altered: the Americans landed at Normandy in June, and the Russians liberated Lublin-Maidanek in July. The inevitability of military defeat and the threat of punishment for war crimes led Himmler and other high-ranking Nazis to offer the release of Jews for ransom in money or goods, or postwar alibis. The creation of the War Refugee Board in January 1944 resulted in limited American financing for rescue operations in Europe, despite the Treasury embargo on trade with the Axis. Public opinion forced the Swiss government to relax the stringent implementation of border regulations, which had previously denied asylum to Jewish refugees. After the German occupation of Hungary in March 1944 both private and semiofficial emissaries tried to rescue the Jews of Hungary by negotiating with the SS. Joel Brand's mission to Istanbul and Syria to swap trucks for Jewish lives was aborted when the British arrested him (see Volume 15 of this series). The negotiations of Rudolph Kasztner, the executive director of the Budapest branch of the Relief and Rescue Committee, with the SS officers Dieter Wisliceny and Kurt Becher, were somewhat more successful, resulting in the release of several wealthy Hungarian Jews to Switzerland and Portugal in exchange for their business holdings. Kasztner developed a mutually beneficial relationship with Becher, who had a direct line to Heinrich Himmler. This proved useful in subsequent negotiations by Saly Mayer with Becher and the parallel negotiations between Jean-Marie Musy and SS Brigadier-General Walter Schellenberg. The Mayer and Musy discussions resulted in the release of approximately three thousand Jews from Bergen-Belsen and Theresienstadt to Switzerland between August 1944 and February 1945.

Saly Mayer (1882–1950) was a Swiss lace and knitwear manufacturer until he retired and sold his business in the 1930s. He served on the St. Gallen Municipal Council from 1921 to 1933. He was an observant Jew, active in communal Jewish organizations. He served as chairman of the Swiss Association of Jewish Communities from 1936 to 1942. After 1940 he worked as the unsalaried representative of the American Jewish Joint Distribution Committee.

In the dilatory negotiations that began on August 20, 1944, on the bridge at St. Margarethen at the Swiss-Austrian border, Saly Mayer represented the Swiss Fund for the Support of Refugees, a cover to hide his affiliation with the American Jewish Joint Distribution Committee. Mayer was discreetly aided by Marcus Wyler, his lawyer; Pierre Bigar, a member of the Swiss Jewish Communities Council; and Roswell McClelland, a former Quaker relief worker in France, who was in 1944 the American War Refugee Board representative in Switzerland. The German delegation consisted of Becher; SS Captain Max Grüson; Wilhelm Billitz, the German appointed to direct the Weiss-Manfred works; and Rudolph Kasztner. With several alterations in personnel these delegations met many times from August 1944 to early February 1945, first at the border and later in Switzerland. The negotiations consisted of a series of delaying tactics in a game of double bluff: the SS negotiators demanded trucks, industrial goods, and money in exchange for not deporting Jews; they had no authority to grant this. Mayer promised a Swiss bank account of several million dollars for such German purchases; the money was actually unavailable. With the Allies closing in, the Nazis probably continued negotiations only to extricate themselves, and Mayer did obtain the release of 1,686 Hungarian Jews from Bergen-Belsen to Switzerland in August and December 1944. The authorized five million US dollars in Joint Distribution Committee funds was spent in early 1945 for food and medicine distributed through the Red Cross in Nazi camps. These controversial and somewhat confused negotiations have remained a subject of historical controversy and polemics to the present.

Jean-Marie Musy (1876–1952) was a Swiss Catholic conservative politician who worked in the Greyzer Finance and Customs Department and was president of the Federal Council in 1925 and 1930. He collaborated with the National Front, producing Nazi films like *Die rote Pest* and publishing the Swiss pro-Nazi newspaper *La Jeune Suisse*. Acting in the name of Agudath Israel and the Committee of Orthodox Rabbis in the United States (the Sternbuch brothers), Musy travelled to Germany in October 1944 and January 1945 to negotiate the release of Jews with Himmler and Schellenberg. As a result of these discussions a train of twelve hundred Jews left Theresienstadt for Switzerland in early February 1945. This intervention created a political alibi for Musy in the aftermath of the war.

The Mayer and Musy negotiations were limited successes. They also prepared the basis for Himmler's later negotiations with Norbert Masur and Count Folke Bernadotte of Sweden, which provided limited last-minute aid for camp inmates. With the exception of Kurt Becher the Germans did not extricate themselves from postwar prosecution. The Hungarian rescue was a limited success story made possible by the changes in American policy through the War Refugee Board and the recognition by SS leaders of their imminent military defeat.

The documents in this volume from the War Refugee Board include the correspondence, cables, and reports of Roswell McClelland and Saly Mayer with the departments of state, war, treasury, and other US diplomatic personnel in allied countries. The Nuernberg Trials prosecution documents include interrogations of Jean-Marie Musy and Kurt Becher from 1945 and 1948. Supplementary archival materials on Saly Mayer and the Joint Distribution Committee are available at the Joint Distribution Committee Archives in New York. Further material on Musy and Saly Mayer are also found in the Sternbuch papers at the Agudath Israel Archive in New York. Several historical monographs complete the historical background: for the story of Hungarian Jews, see Randolph L. Braham, *The Politics of Genocide: The Holocaust in Hungary*, 2 volumes (New York: Columbia University Press, 1981), especially vol. 2, pp. 922–1026; for American refugee policy and the background of the War Refugee Board, see Henry L. Feingold, *The Politics of Rescue: The Roosevelt Administration and the Holocaust, 1938–1945* (New Brunswick, New Jersey: Rutgers University Press, 1970), and Arthur D. Morse, *While Six Million Died: A Chronicle of American Apathy* (New York: Ace, 1967); for the rescue work of the Joint Distribution Committee and the Saly Mayer story, see Yehuda Bauer, *American Jewry and the Holocaust: the American Jewish Joint Distribution Committee, 1939–1945* (Detroit: Wayne State University Press, 1981), and Yad Vashem, *Rescue Attempts During the Holocaust: Proceedings of the Second Yad Vashem International Historical Conference, April 8–11, 1974* (Jerusalem: Yad Vashem, 1977); and for Switzerland, see Alfred A. Häsler, *The Lifeboat is Full: Switzerland and the Refugees, 1933–1945*, translated by Charles Lam Markmann (New York: Funk and Wagnalls, 1969). For a comprehensive survey of rescue documentation in the National Archives, see John Mendelsohn, "The Holocaust: Rescue and Relief Documentation in the National Archives," in *The Annals of the American Academy of Political and Social Science*, vol. 450 (July 1980), pp. 237–249.

Sybil Milton

SOURCE ABBREVIATIONS
AND DESCRIPTIONS

Nuernberg Document

Records from five of the twenty-five Nuernberg Trials prosecution document series: the NG (Nuernberg Government) series, the NI (Nuernberg Industrialist) series, the NO (Nuernberg Organizations) series, the NOKW (Nuernberg Armed Forces High Command) series, and the PS (Paris-Storey) series. Also included are such Nuernberg Trials prosecution records as interviews, interrogations, and affidavits, excerpts from the transcripts of the proceedings, briefs, judgments, and sentences. These records were used by the prosecution staff of the International Military Tribunal at Nuernberg or the twelve United States military tribunals there, and they are part of National Archives Record Group 238, National Archives Collection of World War II War Crimes Records.

OSS

Reports by the Office of Strategic Services in National Archives Record Group 226.

SEA

Staff Evidence Analysis: a description of documents used by the Nuernberg prosecution staff. Although the SEA's tended to describe only the evidentiary parts of the documents in the summaries, they describe the document title, date, and sources quite accurately.

State CDF

Central Decimal File: records of the Department of State in National Archives Record Group 59, General Records of the Department of State.

T 120

Microfilm Publication T 120: records of the German foreign office received from the Department of State in Record Group 242, National Archives Collection of Foreign Records Seized, 1941–. The following citation system is used for National Archives

Microfilm Publications: The Microfilm Publication number followed by a slash, the roll number followed by a slash, and the frame number(s). For example, Document 1 in Volume I: T 120/4638/K325518—K325538.

T 175	Microfilm Publication T 175: records of the Reich leader of the SS and of the chief of the German police in Record Group 242.
U.S. Army and U.S. Air Force	Records relating to the attempts to cause the U.S. Army Air Force to bomb the extermination facilities at Auschwitz and the railroad center at Kaschau leading to Auschwitz, which are part of a variety of records groups and collections in the National Archives. Included are records of the United States Strategic Bombing Survey (Record Group 243), records of the War Refugee Board (Record Group 220), records of the Joint Chiefs of Staff, and other Army record collections.
War Refugee Board	Records of the War Refugee Board, located at the Franklin D. Roosevelt Library in Hyde Park, New York. They are part of National Archives Record Group 220, Records of Temporary Committees, Commissions and Boards. Included in this category are the papers of Myron C. Taylor and Ira Hirschmann.

CONTENTS

Notes

1. *Document 1.* SS *Standartenfuehrer* Kurt Becher headed the economic staff of the SS operational command in Hungary; Otto Winkelmann was the higher SS and police leader in Hungary; Walter Schellenberg was the chief of the combined civil and military intelligence service of the Reich Security Main Office of the SS. Ernst Kaltenbrunner was the successor of Reinhardt Heydrich as chief of the Reich Security Main Office. The International Military Tribunal at Nuernberg sentenced him to death, and he was executed in Nuernberg in 1946.

2. *Document 2.* Roswell D. McClelland was the representative of the War Refugee Board in Switzerland. Jean-Marie Musy was a counsellor in Switzerland.

3. *Document 4.* Brigadier General William O'Dwyer succeeded John W. Pehle as executive director of the War Refugee Board.

4. *Document 5.* Leland Harrison was the American envoy at the legation in Bern.

5. *Document 6.* Henry R. Norweb was the American ambassador in Lisbon; Joseph Schwartz was the representative of the Joint Distribution Committee there.

6. *Document 11.* Edward R. Stettinius was secretary of state from December 1, 1944; before that he served as deputy secretary of state. Saly Mayer was the Swiss representative of the American Jewish Joint Distribution Committee.

7. *Document 11.* Robert F. Kelley was chargé d'affaires at the American embassy in Ankara.

8. *Document 12.* Cordell Hull was secretary of state until November 30, 1944.

9. *Document 15.* Moses A. Leavitt was secretary of the American Jewish Joint Distribution Committee.

10. *Document 21.* Robert Pilpel was the acting European director of the American Jewish Joint Distribution Committee.

11. *Document 33.* Hershel V. Johnson was American envoy extraordinary in Stockholm.

12. *Document 49.* Jerome K. Huddle was a counsellor at the American legation in Bern.

Vernehmung des Kurt Becher
vom 22. 6. 1948 von 1400-1500
durch Mr. Barr
Stenographin Frl. Helma Schmidt

1. F. Ich moechte nun noch einmal von Ihnen die Geschichte dargestellt haben.

A. Muesy war mit Himmler irgendwie bekannt. Er wandte sich an Himmler, dass
er sich da einschalten wollte. Man wollte das aber nicht. Dann Schrieb
Muesy wieder an Himmler im Dezember wegen zwei oder drei Juden. Er fragte,
ob er nicht eingeschaltet werden koenne in die grosse Sache. Er koenne
Cibazol und andere pharmazeutische Artikel liefern. Himmler zeigte mir
das. Er hat einen Lachkrampf bekommen. Er wollte doch 10.000 Lastwagen
haben. Er hat mir das als ein Kuriosum gezeigt. Er fragte:"Was soll
ich mit dem alten Deppen machen? Ich kann ihn ja mal kommen lassen".
Zu irgend einem Zeitpunkt, als die Sache Muesy schon wieder ganz erledigt
war und ich ein paar Tage vorher bei Himmler gewesen war um die Genehmigung
zu erhalten, in die Schweiz zu reisen, telefonierte ich nochmals mit
Grothmann. Der sagte mir, ich solle nochmals vorher zu Himmler kommen,
ehe ich abfahre. Ich fuhr hin und sprach telephonisch mit Grothmann. Er sagte mir, ich solle mit SCHELLENBERG sprechen. Der sagte mir, dass er bei
der Besprechung MUESY dabei gewesen sei. SCHELLENBERG war der Mann, der
die auslaendischen Gaeste empfing. SCHELLENBERG sagte mir: " Aus der Sache
haben sich fuer mich Perspektiven ergeben, die mich veranlassen, mich in
die Sache einzuschalten." Ich fragte,"was fuer welche ". Er antwortete mir:
" Ich kriege in den naechsten 14 Tagen in den 8 fuehrendsten Zeitungen positive Artikel. Das wuerde fuer HIMMLER schlagartig in der internationalen Be-
urteilung eine andere Atmosphaere schaffen." Ich fragte: "Glauben Sie das?"
Er sagte: " Selbstverstaendlich. Das ist eine absolut serioese Sache". "Sie
werden sehen, dass in den naechsten 14 Tagen die Zeitungen davon voll sein
werden." Ich konnte das nicht glauben, denn ich kannte ja die Einstellung
des Joint. Ich kannte ja die Schwierigkeiten, die zwischen der Joint und
HIMMLER bestanden, und ich wusste, dass HIMMLER immer noch auf seine Lastwagen wartete. Ich sagte deshalb: "Es wird sehr schwierig sein, wenn man
das zusammen bringen soll".

Doc. 1

1

Darauf sagte SCHELLENBERG: "Dann muss eben einer ausscheiden". Er sagte:
" Dann muessen Sie eben ausscheiden ". Er sagte: "Das geht Ihrer Sache voraus.
Es handelt sich da um eine ganz entscheidende Aktion."Ich fragte, ob das der
Reichsfuehrer entschieden haette. Es hiess "Nein". Ich fuhr am naechsten Tag
zu HIMMLER, zusammen mit WINKELMANN. SCHELLENBERG war auch da. HIMMLER hat
mich allein empfangen. Ich habe ihm gesagt, dass ich ihm doch berichtet haette, dass die Joint keinen Sinn darin sehe, wenn MUESY eingeschaltet sei, denn
bisher war ja von der politischen Zeitungsgeschichte nicht die Rede gewesen.
Darauf sagte mir HIMMLER: "Gut, machen Sie Ihre Sache allein, und SCHELLENBERG
macht auch seine Sache allein".

2. F. Das ist ziemlich logisch.

A. HIMMLER hat mich zuerst ziemlich angeschnauzt, etwa in der Art: " Wo denn
meine Leistungen blieben ". HIMMLER sagte: "Wie ist das nun mit diesem Transport". HIMMLER hatte mir einen Transport zugesagt, und ich hatte erfahren,
dass SCHELLENBERG den Transport uebernehmen wolle, oder uebernommen hatte. -
Ich halte es da nun fuer absolut moeglich, dass HIMMLER dann zu SCHELLENBERG
gesagt hat: "Das ist Ihr Transport". Als ich in die Schweiz kam, kam mir Sxixx
Sally MEYER entgegen und sagte: "Es ist eine furchtbare Schweinerei. Die Presse ist voll von HIMMLER-MUESY und MUESY-HIMMLER. Die Links- und die Rechtspres-
se streitet sich. Was ist denn los, um Gottes Willen. Wir hatten doch verein-
bart, die Sache geheim zu halten. Ich hatte auch immer HIMMLER gesagt: "Es
geht nur, wenn es ganz verschwiegen gemacht wird". Ich wusste ja seit August,
dass die Lastwagen nicht kommen. MEYER sagte zu mir: " Wenn wir Presse haetten
bringen wollen, haetten wir das besser gekonnt als Herr MUESY. " Das waren die
wichtigsten Punkte der Besprechung. Nun kommt die Reaktion. Ich komme zu
HIMMLER. Vorher hoerte ich schon, dass HIMMLER wahnsinnig boese sei, angeblich
auf mich. GROTHMANN sagte mir: " Wenn Sie nichts Wichtiges haben, bleiben Sie
lieber weg. Der Reichsfuehrer ist sehr boese." Ich ging trotzdem hin und sagte:
"Reichsfuehrer, Sie sind boese?" Er sagte: "Nein, nicht auf Sie. Ich bin veraergert, weil durch die verdammten Schweinereien in der Presse der Schweiz
der Fuehrer dahinter gekommen ist, und verboten hat, dass irgendwelche Juden
ausgeliefert werden.

3. F. Waren Sie bei der Konferenz anwesend ?

   A. HIMMLER und HITLER? Nein.

4. F. KALTENBRUNNER / HIMMLER in diesem Zusammenhang?

   A. Nein. - Ich bin aus der Schweiz zurueckgekommen und wollte sofort wieder zu HIMMLER.

5. F. War das nach der Konferenz?

   A. Nein, das war noch bevor mir HIMMLER sagte, dass HITLER die Sache verboten habe. Das war etwa am 10. Februar. Ich wollte HIMMLER sprechen auf Grund meiner Unterredung mit Sally. Das wurde sehr geschickt abgebogen, indem ich mich mit SCHELLENBERG und KALTENBRUNNER und WINKELMANN - auf dessen Anwesenheit hatte ich bestanden - unterhalten sollte. Auf Aus dieser Unterhaltung bin ich nie ganz schlau geworden.

6. F. Ich kann mir gar nicht vorstellen, dass sich die Leute so schlau benommen haben.

   A. Es war nicht zu erkennen, ob KALTENBRUNNER und SCHELLENBERG miteinanderzogen oder gegneinander. KALTENBRUNNER versuchte die Rolle zu spielen, SCHELLENBERG und mich zu koordinieren. SCHELLENBERG versuchte, mich zu diskrimieren, indem er sagte : "Seien Sie still. Sie haben sich von Sally MEYER das letzte Mal 20 000 Franken geben lassen." Ich war ganz platt und konnte nichts sagen. WINKELMANN wurde boes. KALTENBRUNNER sagte: "Das ist laecherlich. Ueber solchen Mist brauchen wir nicht zu reden." SCHELLENBERG sagte: "Das haben mir meine Nachrichtenleute berichtet." SCHELLENBERG versuchte sich also herauszureden, indem er sagte, er koenne ja nicht nachpruefen, was ihm berichtet wuerde. Dann kam ein Fliegeralarm dazwischen und KALTENBRUNNER sagte: "Dann sollen die Leute in der Schweiz entscheiden, mit wem sie weiterarbeiten wollen, ob mit SCHELLENBERG oder mit BECHER. Dann sagte ich: "Ich fahre morgen zu HIMMLER".

7. F. Sie haben mit KALTENBRUNNER nicht allein gesprochen ?

   A. Nein. - Diese Unterredung war anfangs Februar. Es waren anwesend: KALTENBRUNNER, WINKELMANN, XX SCHELLENBERG und ich. Ich wollte zu HIMMLER. WINKELMANN sagte mir, ich solle nicht zu HIMMLER fahren. WINKELMANN versprach mir aber noch zu HIMMLER zu gehen. Als ich dann zurueckkam, hiess es: Beim Reichsfuehrer ist grosser Krach. Bleiben Sie im Hintergrund. Ich sagte: "Nein, ich fahre zu HIMMLER." Dann sagte mir HIMMLER auf meine

3

Frage: " Ich habe nichts gegen Sie. Ich bin veraergert wegen des

"Kuddelmuddels. "

4

Testimony of Jean Marie Musy, taken at Berne,
Switzerland, on 26 October 1945, by Major Robert
Haythorne, OUSCC.
Commenced at 4:10 PM - Ended at 5:15 PM

TO THE INTERPRETER by Major Haythorne:

Q   What is your full name?

A   Roswell D. McClelland.

Q   What is your present position?

A   I am an auxiliary officer attached to the American Legation, Berne.

Q   Do you solemnly swear that you will faithfully translate from English
into French, and from French into English, the testimony given here today, so help
you God?

A   I do.

TO THE WITNESS through the interpreter, by Major Haythorne:

Q   Do you swear that the testimony you are about to give will be the truth,
the whole truth, and nothing but the truth, so help you God?

A   Yes.

Q   What is your name?

A   Jean Marie Musy.

Q   How old are you?

A   76.

Q   Mr. Musy, I understand that you had some activities in connection with
an attempt to get people from concentration camps in Germany, to be delivered by
the Germans and transported to Switzerland. I should like to ask you a few questions
in connection with that.

- 1 -   (MUSY)

A   I never had any other connection with Germany except during the war.

Q   In connection with your activities in securing people from the concentration camps, when did you take your first step?

A   The first time I intervened was at Paris, in the month of June 1944, for a young man from Fribourg whose brother was in the same squadron as my son, who was in Florida.

Q   At that time to whom did you speak?

A   The intervention was with the head of the Gestapo in Paris, Ober, concerning this girl in Fribourg, named Loeb, for whom I intervened in June 1944. I was able to obtain her liberation after lengthy negotiations with this man.

Q   Did you deal, at this time, with anybody except the head of the Gestapo in Paris?

A   No. Never. Only with Ober. I didn't know this man Ober.

Q   What was the next occasion on which you interceded?

A   A month later I was approached by a woman in Lausanne, in the month of July 1944, who was a friend of my wife's.

Q   What was her name?

A   Torel. Her son had been arrested by the Germans. I tried to see the Gestapo head in Paris but was not successfull.

Q   What was the next time that you interceded?

A   When I returned from Paris, having been unsuccessful, the woman in question begged me to go to Berlin. Mrs. Torel belonged to the Matoassin family. (Bulgarians)

Q   Did you go to Berlin?

- 2 -   (MUSY)

A   I wrote to Himmler, whom I had met on one or two occasions sometime before the war in meetings concerning Communism.

Q   Had you discussed the matter of getting people out of Germany, with Himmler, before this time?

A   No. I wrote to Himmler and explained to him about the situation of this young man whose family was anguished concerning his fate, and asked if I could come and see him about it.

Q   What was Himmler's reply?

A   He said he would see me. Himmler answered, "yes," and specified the date. This took place toward the end of October. On All Saint's Day I was at Berlin.

Q   Before this time, had Mrs. Sternbuch said anything to you about these matters?

A   Yes. Regarding Jews.

Q   When did Mrs. Sternbuch first talk to you about Jews?

A   The first time it was not she who came. It was a woman from Lausanne who came to me.

Q   Do you remember the name of that woman?

A   I don't remember her name. She was a friend of Mrs. Torel.

Q   Did this lady from Lausanne come on behalf of Mrs. Sternbuch?

A   She came to me for Mrs. Sternbuch.

Q   What did she request of you?

A   This lady told me that she was in touch with a woman who was very much concerned about the fate of Jews in camps in Germany, and knowing that I had effected the release of people, begged me to meet her friend, Mrs. Sternbuch. I finally agreed and Mr. and Mrs. Sternbuch came, and some other people whose names

- 3 -   (MUSY)

I do not recall. This Mrs. Sternbuch had her father and mother, and brothers and sisters. She was particularly interested in seeing her father and mother, again. The parents had been at Drancy and later at Vittel.

Q   What was the date when you saw Mr. & Mrs. Sternbuch?

A   These people came to see me about the middle of the month of October, at Fribourg.

Q   Did you do anything or take any action as a result of this meeting?

A   These people came to see me before I received an answer from Himmler, but I had already made up my mind to go.

Q   What was Himmler's reply?

A   He had an answer sent to me that he was disposed to receive me.

Q   Who signed the letter?

A   The letter came through the German Legation. I do not remember who signed the letter.

Q   Did the letter say when and where he would receive you?

A   It did not specify the time or place, but merely said that if I wish to see Himmler, I should come to Berlin.

Q   How long after you received the letter was it before you left for Berlin?

A   I left about a week later.

Q   When you arrived at Berlin, who was the first person you attempted to see in connection with that?

A   When I crossed the border at Constance I was informed by the German Customs that I was expected, and a man was appointed to conduct me to Berlin, since the roads were uncertain already at that time.

Q   What was this man's name?

A   I don't remember.

- 4 -   (MUSY)

Q   Did this man take you directly to Himmler?

A   He took us to Berlin. My son was driving the car. He took us to a spot near the offices, I assume, of the International Red Cross, and it was there that I met Schellenberg for the first time, whom I did not know then.

Q   Did you explain your business to Schellenberg?

A   I explained to Schellenberg what my business was. Schellenberg answered that, "Himmler will receive you tomorrow or the next day, and I will take you to him."

Q   When did he take you to Himmler?

A   Schellenberg told me that the only person who could do anything about getting people out of camps was Himmler, and therefore it was necessary to see him.

Q   Several days later, did Schellenberg take you to see Himmler?

A   Two days later Schellenberg took me in the vicinity of Breslau. There I got on Himmler's train.

Q   How many meetings or conversations did you have with Himmler on this subject at this time?

A   I had only one conversation with Himmler at that time, and I had only two conversations in all.

Q   What did you say to Himmler?

A   I asked Himmler to liberate Torel, and all the Jews who were confined in concentrationcamps for religious reasons. Not just Mrs. Sternbuch's relatives.

Q   What did Himmler say in reply?

A   Himmler was very comprehensive. It was not easy to convince him. I told him, "You have lost the war."

- 5 -   (MUSY)

9

Q   "hat were Himmler's objections?

A   Naturally Himmler raised objections, since the elimination of the Jews was one of the bases of National Socialism. I explained to him, however, that they had not sworn to kill the Jews and, therefore, they should have no objection to getting rid of them. The first time I did not tell him, "You have lost the war," but rather, "You will not win the war."

Q   Did Himmler raise any practical difficulties, such as transportation or administration?

A   He did raise objections of a practical nature, but I told him there was an American organization which would be willing to assist in the transportation and they, the Germans, should do something about it themselves. We discussed the matter during at least two hours, at the end of which Himmler declared himself ready, at my insistence, to liberate all the Jews.

Q   Was any specific agreement reached at that time for the picking up and transporting of the Jews?

A   Yes, it was. Himmler said they are ready to liberate these people and transport and feed them, as far as the border, but they would have to have material compensation such as trucks and tractors.

Q   Did he mention money?

A   I pointed out to him that it would be extremely difficult to obtain trucks, etc, because of the Allies; and that it would probably be easier to secure money as Sternbuch had mentioned the possibility to me of obtaining large sums. Himmler did not wish to entirely abandon the idea of compensation in goods, and asked me to try for that, but if I was not successful, that a compromise might be effected on the subject of foreign exchange. He said they would start immediately with the liberation of Jews.

(MUSY)

Q   Himmler's original thought wasthat you would give these trucks and tractors to Germany, and not just to use them for the transportation of the people, is that right,

A   It was for Germany, and not to transport these people.

Q   Who else was present at this conference?

A   Nobody else was present.

Q   Was the conference heldina building, or in the car onhis train?

A   It was held in his private car. I can say that I am sure if Himmler had been alone in the matter, they would have liberated all the Jews.

Q   Specifically, at the end of the meeting, what was the agreement between you and Himmler?

A   Then the conclusion of the arrangement was that Himmler would abandon the question of "goods" compensation and accept that of foreign exchange. His tone was that he had enough of the entire Jewish questionand that they could have them all.

Q   Was an amount of foreign exchange settled on at that meeting?

A   At that time I did not.

Q   Under what circumstances was that meeting terminated?. At what time of day, and what did you do after the meeting?

A   I left Himmler's private car and returned onthe train with Schellenberg.

Q   Himmler's agreement then was that he would do nothing until he further heard from you, is that correct?

A   No, that is not correct. They said that they would go ahead. It was only later, in Switzerland, that it was agreed that a specific sum of 5 million francs would be forthcoming from the Union of Rabbis, and that this sum, however, would be turned over to the German Red Cross to be used for the relief of German civilian population.

- 7 -   (MUSY)

This was at my suggestion, since I pointed out to Himmler that the whole affair should not have an aura of slave trading.

Q   To go back to the meeting with Himmler, was his conclusion that he would deliver the Jews regardless of compensation, and in the meanwhile you would try to arrange some sort of a money payment?

A   That is correct, although the question of compensation really no longer played a capital role.

Q   Did Himmler say when, where, or how, he would deliver these people?

A   He said they would begin right away, via Constance.

Q   Were any Jewish people released and delivered to Constance as he said?

A   Yes. The first convoy, consisting of 1200 people from Theresienstadt.

Q   When were they delivered?

A   Early in February 1945.

Q   Were any more people delivered, according to Himmler's statement?

A   Young Torel was liberated, and two brothers of Mrs. Sternbuch, since they had not been able to find her father and mother, who had been sent to Auschwitz, and were probably dead.

Q   Why were no more people delivered than the first convoy and these few extra individuals?

A   Although I do not know exactly, this seems to have been due to the intercessions of Saly Meyer.

12

Further testimony of Jean Marie Musy, taken at Berne,
Switzerland, on 29 October 1945, by Major Robert Haythorne,
OUSCC.
Commenced at 10 AM - Ended at 12:15 PM

The witness was reminded that he was still under oath, and testified through interpreter
in French, as follows:

Q   Mr. Musy, I direct your mind back to the first conference you had with
Himmler, and just as you left Himmler at his train. Let us carry the story of what
you did from there. What is the first thing you did, and where did you go, after you
left the private train of Himmler?

A   I returned to Berlin where Torel turned up, and then I went back to Switzerland
in order to see whether anything could be done about compensation in goods, although I
realized myself that this was hopeless.

Q   How many days after you left Himmler was it before you returned to Switzerland?

A   Three or four days.

Q   In those three or four days, did you discuss with any German officials the
same material that you had discussed with Himmler?

A   I did not discuss this matter with any other persons.

Q   When you returned to Switzerland, with whom did you discuss this compensation
problem?

A   I had a meeting with the Sternbuch's and with Mrs. Bolomet, from Lausanne, who
had originally introduced Mrs. Sternbuch to me. I also had discussions with the Ciba
Concern, in Basle, regarding the possibility of securing pharmaceutical equipment for
possible compensation in operations.

- 1 -   (MUSY)

Q   At this first meeting then, whenyou returned from Germany, there were present Mr. & Mrs. Sternbuch, Madam Bolomet and yourself. Were there any other people there?

A   No.

Q   Can you recall approximately the date of this meeting?

A   Around the 20th of November.

Q   Were you able to arrange any method of obtaining material considerations, such as goods, to be givento the Germans?

A   No. Nothing really definite was arranged. Mrs. Bolomet, as far as I recall, even undertook a trip to Paris to discuss the questionwith certain Allied authorities there. Mrs. Sternbuch later telephoned me to state thatx the result of such negotiations would take a considerable time. They couldn't wait that long.

Q   How many meetings did you have with these people in this general space of time, onthis same question of consideration?

A   I do not know exactly, but several meetings; since they were always after me.

Q   What conclusions did you reach through these meetings, and what did you thendecide to do?

A   There were no definite conclusions other thanthe fact that I should return and continue discussions. Mrs. Sternbuch was still most insistent onthe subject of her parents, as well as the general questionof rescuing Jews.

Q   Had the meetings resulted in any conclusion as to what could be offered in the way of considerationto the Germans?

A   Our conclusion was that the questionof obtaining goods would last far too long and that on returning I would have to inform Himmler that he would have to be satisfied with currency or cash.

- 2 -   (MUSY)

Q   Did you discuss from whom the cash was to come, how much you would be prepared to offer to Himmler, and inwhat manner the payment should be made?

A   No specific sum was mentioned. Sternbuch, however, led me to believe that he had been able to obtain sizable amounts of money from the Union of Orthodox Rabbis in the United States. The plan would be to transfer this money to Switzerland. They askedme to try to get out of Himmler what amount he considered adequate, and they would see what they could do about it.

Q   Did you make another trip to Germany?

A   Yes.

Q   When did you make this trip?

A   About the middle of December.

Q   Did you write a letter, requesting an interview?

A   Yes, I did. I wrote a letter to Himmler.

Q   What was Himmler's replyto your letter?

A   The answer from Berlin through the German Legation in Berne was that he would receive money. I left three or four days later.

Q   Did you drive to Berlin?

A   Yes. Always.

Q   When you reached Berlin, did you see Himmler?

A   Himmler was not at Berlin. He was in the western part of Germany.

Q   Did you discuss this business with anybody in Berlin?

A   I discussed it with Schellenberg who always xhowed himself ready to assist in this questionof liberating concentration camp inmates.

- 3 -   (MUSY)

15

Q   What was your impression of how much authority Schellenberg had in this

matter?

A   It was never quite clear to me, the extent of Schellenberg's authority in

such questions. I could only say that he did his best to arrange the matter, and

I have the impressionthat in the last analysis such matters were directly controlled

by Hitler.

Q   Did Schellenberg ever tell you that,he would do anything about the matter,

or did you ever hear him speak to Himmler or Hitler about it?

A   Schellenberg did not promise to do anything onhis own, specifically, beyond

doing all he could to help my efforts with Himmler, to accomplish the liberation of

people. At the time of my second interview with Himmler, Schellenberg was present

and attempted repeatedly to persuade Himmler to undertake the desired action.

16

Q   On your second visit to Berlin, and before you saw Himmler, did you discuss

this matter with anyone except Schellenberg?

A   No.

Q   Did Schellenberg take you to Himmler?

A   Yes.

Q   Where did you see Himmler then?

A   I do not know the exact time or place, but it was in the Black Forest,

several hundred kilometers to the southwest of Berlin.

Q   When you met Himmler, was the meeting in a building, in a train, or in an

automobile, or just where?

A   It took place in a hotel.

- 4 -   (MUSY)

Q   On this occasion how many conversations did you have with Himmler?

A   A single long conversation.

Q   At what time of day?

A   In the evening.

Q   Who else was present at this conversation?

A   Himmler, Schellenberg and myself. That is all. Himmler informed me that according to his knowledge, the Union of Orthodox Rabbis was not a particularly important or representative body in the United States and that he understood the organization which Saly Meyer represented, in Switzerland, was more important (The American Joint Distribution Committee.). He told me that this matter would have to be cleared up. On returning to Switzerland, therefore, I told Sternbuch about this and he telegraphed his organization, which sent back an answer stating that they were infact an influential body among Jews in the United States and that they underlined the fact that Sternbuch was solely authorized to deal for them in this matter.

Q   To return to your meeting with Himmler. What was your original comment to him about the subject? At what point did the discussion begin?

A   Himmler immediately brought up this question of Saly Meyer. At the start of this conversation I offered to withdraw if he preferred to deal with Saly Meyer, but he said, "No, since you are here we will continue our discussion under the reservation, however, that this matter will be cleared up." I, therefore, presented to him a list of several individuals, Swiss, non-Jewish, whose liberation was desired by persons in Switzerland.

Q   Did you discuss the point of consideration at this time?

17

A   I pointed out to Himmler that the question of compensation in goods was completely impossible. He, therefore, agreed that money would be acceptable instead and in general was far more accommodating in the whole affair, and seemed to be willing to allow these people to leave. I pointed out to him that he should not give the impression of trafficking in human lives against money, but should rather attempt to exploit the political advantages of such a move.

Q   Was any sum of money designated at this time?

A   No.

Q   Was anything said about obtaining publicity for the releasing of these people?

A   Yes. That was one of the conditions made, that the press in the United States comment favorably.

Q   During this conversation did you discuss the problem generally, or did you limit it only to the list of names that you presented to Himmler at the beginning?

A   It was a question not only of this list of individuals, but of Jews in general and especially Mrs. Sternbuch's relatives.

Q   What did Himmler say about the list of persons that you gave him, and Mrs. Sternbuch's relatives?

A   He said that he was in agreement to release the Swiss; that they would attempt to find Mrs. Sternbuch's parents, and pending the location of the latter, her two brothers would be released.

Q   Did he say definitely that he would do everything possible immediately to release these people?

A   Yes.

Q   Did he indicate when this might be done, or where the people might be delivered?

A   He took note of the matter and said that instructions would be given first to find the people, and secondly to deliver them to Constance.

Q   Did you ever hear him give orders to someone else on that subject?

(MUSY)

A   I believe he telephoned at the time, although I cannot be certain of more than that he wrote it down.

Q   Were any of these people liberated?

A   Yes. The two brothers of Mrs. Sternbuch; the Graf family of Lausanne (four persons); I asked Himmler on this occasion if he could commission Schellenberg to occupy himself for the liberation of these individuals. Himmler agreed. I considered this a good sign.

Q   Did you ever hear Himmler tell Schellenberg, or did Schellenberg indicate to you that he had been commissioned to work on this matter?

A   Yes. Himmler stated in my presence that Schellenberg would concern himself in this matter.

Q   With respect to the people you named, who were liberated, was any consideration paid?

A   No.

Q   Was Schellenberg commissioned to assist in the liberation of all the Jews, or just those people who were named by you?

A   Yes.

Q   With respect to the question, in general, of the release of all the Jews, what did Himmler say?

A   Himmler agreed, yes, to actively pursue the question of liberating Jews in general.

Q   Did he state anything specifically along the lines of what exactly he would do about it?

A   He said that he would deliver all the Jews.

Q   Did he say when, and where, or how he would do it?

A   Via Constance, through Switzerland.

Q When?

A Right away.

Q Were any of these Jews delivered as he said they would be?

A No. Outside of the people mentioned, nobody was immediately released.

Q Is my understanding right then that at this time Himmler stated that the consideration was unimportant?

A Your understanding is correct. I was later informed, through Schellenberg, that a sum of 5 million Swiss francs would be available in Switzerland in Sternbuch's name, over which I could also exercise some control, and that after the first group of Jews arrived this money would be turned over by me to the International Red Cross in favor of the needy German civilian population. Actually, the sum of 5 million francs was deposited with a banking house in Basle over which I was trustee. I later learned that this money was apparently withdrawn by Sternbuch without my authorization. I intend to take this matter up again with Sternbuch so that I may be covered.

Q Directing your attention back to the meeting with Himmler, when it was finished, what did you do?

A My son and I returned to Switzerland by automobile in order to obtain this necessary declaration of American organizations. Himmler also granted me the liberation of 60 to 70 so-called illegal Jews in Hungary (i.e.: People who have not announced themselves to the authorities.) They later entered Switzerland.

Q Before you returned to Switzerland, did you have any conversations on this subject with Schellenberg?

A No.

Q Did you raise the question of the Hungarian Jews with Himmler, or did he mention that to you?

A The matter of these illegal Jews, as far as I can remember, was suggested by Himmler.

- 8 -   (MUSY)

Q   After your return to Switzerland and when you obtained the wire from the
Jewish organization in the United States, how did you transmit that to Himmler?

A   This message was transmitted to the chief of the German police in the
Constance region, who sent it onby courier to Schellenberg inBerlin.

Q   When did Schellenberg mention the sum of 5 million Swiss francs to you?

A   Schellenberg replied that this question of competence of organizations was
noted, and specified the depositing of the 5 million francs.

Q   Was this a reply to the wire from America, which you sent up to Germany?

A   Schellenberg never directly acknowledged the receipt of my telegram, and since I
made eight visits inall, to Berlin, I do not recall during which one of these the
specific sum was mentioned. I only remember that the questionof the 5 million francs
was mentioned in conversationwith Schellenberg at a later date, in Berlin.

Q   Did you ever discuss this matter with Himmler again?

A   No. Never. I only saw him twice.

Q   Did you ever discuss it with any German official except Schellenberg?

A   I only discussed this with Schellenberg.

Q   Will you, as well as you can remember, state the dates of your visits to
Berlin, after you returned from your second meeting with Himmler?

A   As far as I can remember, I took two trips in January. The first convoy
of Jews arrived in the first part of February, andI made subsequent trips during February,
March and April, to discuss the question of the liberation of more Jews. I returned
from my last trip xx in the first week in April.

Q   During any of these trips, did you see Hitler, Goering, Goebbels, or
Kaltenbrunner?

21

A   I saw only Schellenberg, and towards the end, Goering, who was apparently charged with concentrationcamps.

Q   Will you state the circumstances under which you met Goering, what was discussed, and what he said about the matters that you talked about with him?

A   I met Goering inSchellenberg's office; Schellenberg having stated that he would call in a man who was acquainted with the practical side of the liberation of people. Goering made an impression upon me as a person who was willing to do what he could.

Q   What did you ask of Goering?

A   I had talks four or five times with Goering.

Q   Did you ever seeGoering without Schellenberg?

A   No.

Q   Did you speak directly to Goering, or did Schellenberg put your name before Goering?

A   I spoke directly to Goering.

Q   Is it true that, in general, you asked Goering to assist in the release of Jews fromconcentration camps?

A   Yes.

Q   What was Goering's reaction to your request?

A   Favorable.

Q   Did he say that he would do something in connection with it; that he would take it up with someone else, or were his remarks to you merely general?

A   Goering's answers were of a general nature with the exception of the specific question of Mrs. Sternbuch's relatives.

Q   Did he state that he, himself, would do anything specific to assist you?

A   His reply was of a general nature, with the exception of Sternbuch's

relatives. He, however, discussed the specific problems of Theresienstadt and

Ravensbruck.

Q   As I understand it, only the Jews from Theresienstadt were freed, as a mass

proposition? What were the objections to any more Jews being freed, or what kept any

greater amount from being liberated?

A   Hitler.

Q   Who said that Hitler prevented this?

A   Schellenberg told me that Hitler did not wish this to happen.

Q   Did anyone besides Schellenberg and Himmler mention the money question to you?

A   No.

Q   Did Goering state that he would speak to Hitler to try td arrange to have

the Jews liberated?

A   No. My general impression was that Goering wished to pretend to be more

important than he really was, since he promised to deliver dertain prisoners to the

border, which he never did.

Q   Have you ever met Kaltenbrunner?

A   No.

Q   Do you have anything more that you wish to say about this material?

A   Himmler gave the orders to liberate Theresienstadt. My son left with

Goering to go there and arrange this matter. When they got there, Kaltenbrunner

opposed the liberation of Theresienstadt. Goering sent a wire to Himmler, who

answered giving specific instructions to liberate the camp. I do not know whether

Kaltenbrunner already had in his possession the general orders of Hitler that no further Jews should be liberated. I have the impression, from what my son told me, that there was a fairly heated discussion between Goering and Kaltenbrunner at Theresienstadt.

Q   Was the result then, that Kaltenbrunner caused Hitler to change his order on the liberation of this camp?

A   I don't know.

Q   How do you know that Kaltenbrunner opposed the liberation of the Jews from Theresienstadt?

A   From my son. When we speak of Theresienstadt now, we are speaking about the liberation of the whole camp, and not the one original shipment that was made in February.

Q   Did you have anything to do with the evacuation of the concentration camps when the American Army advanced to their locations?

A   When Schellenberg informed me that Hitler had given instructions to evacuate all of the concentrationcamps, and it was realized that this would undoubtedly occasion the death of hundreds of thousands of people, after communication with Himmler, Himmler stated that if the Allies would agree to treat the personnel of concentration camps as prisoners of war, and not shoot them, he, Himmler, would be willing to give instructions contrary to Hitler's orders, not to evacuate the concentration camps. This was communicated to me through Schellenberg. Himmler actually gave orders for the camps to be kept intact.

Q   How do you know that?

A   My son, who was at Buchenwald, told me that whenhe was there alone, they had started to evacuate the internees. He remonstrated with the head of the camp and then returned to Berlink in his car, where he told Schellenberg about this. Schellenberg immediately gave instructions that the camp should not be evacuated; that those were Himmler's orders.

Q   Did the Germans ever ask you to transmit a message to the Americans stating that they would keep the inmates in the concentrationcamps if the Americans would promise to treat the guards as prisoners of war?

A   Yes. Schellenberg gave me this request, which I transmitted to the Americans.

Q   Mr. Musy , would you be willing, if it was indicated that your presence was desirable in Nuremberg, to go to Nuremberg and be a witness in the Nuremberg trial?

A   I don't think I could do it. I would need Governmental authorization.

Q   I mean, only your personal desire, if the other material could be arranged?

A   I would prefer not to.

25

LEGATION OF THE
UNITED STATES OF AMERICA

AIR MAIL

Bern, Switzerland
August 2, 1945.

Dear General O'Dwyer:

I am most happy to be able - finally - to forward enclosed herewith, to the Board and to you, two copies of my general report covering the activities of the re-presentation of the W.R.B. at the American Legation in Bern from March 1944 through July 1945. While it is far from being as smooth and consecutive a piece of prose as I should have desired, had I had more time available to work it over, I hope that it contains material which will be of value to you and your colleagues in drawing up your own final reports.

I wish to thank you sincerely for your very generous and warm letter of July 14 with respect to my service under the War Refugee Board during the past fifteen months in Switzerland. I am afraid that you are really giving me credit for far more than my due since our effort in behalf of the victims of Nazi persecution was a collective more than an individual one. I did my best to contribute to this larger endeavor in which all of us, both in the United States and abroad, shared.

I shall be sending the Board one or two more messages in the course of the next few days concerning details of the final wind-up of Board activities which now show good prospect - including _even_ the departure of our refugees - of coming to a successful conclusion in the near future. I am sorry that, in keeping with your desire expressed some weeks ago, it has not been possible to do this sooner.

In closing allow me to send you my kind personal regards, to express my sincere appreciation of your constant confidence in and support of my activities, and to wish you the best in your own future undertakings. Please remember me to Miss Hodel.

Very sincerely yours,

Roswell S. McClelland

Enclosures: 2 copies of
general report.

Brigadier General William O'Dwyer
Executive Director
War Refugee Board,
Washington, D.C.

REPORT ON THE ACTIVITIES OF THE WAR REFUGEE BOARD THROUGH ITS REPRESENTATION AT THE AMERICAN LEGATION IN BERN, SWITZERLAND

March 1944 - July 1945

******

INTRODUCTION

"The explanation of our defeats is that we have not yet begun to fight" wrote Giuseppe Borgese, the Italian critic and philosopher, in the opening line of a recent book. This was dated July 1942.

With respect to the unprecedented campaign of persecution which the Nazis had waged since 1933, first in their own country and later, as the quick succession of conquest brought more and more countries under their domination, in most of Europe, we must truthfully admit that we did not begin to fight until very late. From one point of view it is doubtless to our credit that we did not, and indeed do not generally now, grasp or believe the truly diabolic character of the Nazi revolution and the sinister thoroughness with which its German followers put into practice their domineering philosophy of a master race. The gap between the norms which govern our behavior and the actions of the Nazis is too great for us to comprehend the positive use by a modern state as an accepted practice of government of such instruments as the gas chamber and the concentration camp.

It is the rôle of leaders, however, in their larger awareness of such developments, to think ahead of their people and to initiate action the reasons for which may not be generally realized until some time later. It is illustrative of the prescience of our late great President, Franklin Roosevelt, and of that of some of his close advisers, that he set up in January of 1944, almost a year and a half before Germany went down to final defeat before the armed might of the Allied nations, a special American governmental agency whose one task was the rescue from the Nazis of as many as possible of the persecuted minorities of Europe, whether racial, religious or political. In his executive order Mr. Roosevelt declared:

> "It is the policy of this government to take all measures within its power to rescue the victims of enemy oppression who are in imminent danger of death and otherwise to afford such victims all possible relief and assistance consistent with the successful prosecution of the war."

Thus with the setting-up of the War Refugee Board at the eleventh hour of a night whose remaining minutes were still to afford many opportunities to bring aid and encouragement to at least some of the hundreds of thousands of innocent victims of Nazi savagery the United States began to fight on that particular front. The following pages recount the details of a fight, whose weapons were neither bomb nor bullet, undertaken on a small sector of that larger battlefront.

29

FRANCE

Of all the countries bordering on Switzerland and occupied by Nazi forces perhaps the closest and most well developed contacts existed with France. The French-speaking cantons of Switzerland, particularly Geneva, have always been bound by close cultural, linguistic and economic ties to France. The fact too that some of the French departments adjacent to the Swiss border had been under German control since 1940 meant that intercourse between these regions was well organized. Most of the various French resistance groups had unofficial representatives in Geneva and a number of the international relief agencies had personnel attached to their Swiss offices who had been withdrawn from France at the time of the German occupation of the old "free zone" in November 1942. It was, therefore,

a comparatively easy matter for the Board's representative
in Switzerland (who had himself worked in France with an
American relief committee from 1941 to the middle of 1942,
and had since been active in Geneva) to make use of several
channels to receive information concerning the needs of
endangered refugees and persecuted groups in France and to
plan and initiate whatever WRB relief and rescue work seemed
expedient. Such work was done almost exclusively through
existing organizations such as the Joint Distribution Committee,
the Union O.S.E. (the Jewish children's relief agency), the
Unitarian Service Committee, French YMCA, Spanish "Comité
d'Union National, French "Conseil National de la Résistance -
Social Service Section, and the World Jewish Congress, and
financial aid was the main tool. The pattern of activity was very
much the same as that developed in other European countries.
Funds in Swiss francs which had been received either independently
by the organizations themselves having been transmitted under
special Treasury license from the United States, or in the
case of WRB grants, which came from Board discretionary funds
already in Switzerland, were made available. They were used
to acquire local currency in France either through clearing
schemes or less often by the purchase of French currency in
Switzerland, due care being taken to obtain "clean" money,
which was then smuggled into France.

Since as a general policy it proved safer and more
practical to expand and intensify the effectiveness of measures
of "protective"/relief rather than to attempt the hazardous
work of moving endangered persons many of whom, if foreign
refugees, spoke only broken French, into Spain or Switzerland, funds sent into France both by other agencies and by
the Board served primarily to enable people to better evade
the Gestapo, and SS and its more vicious local counterpart,
the French "Milice."

False papers were the order of the day in France
during the occupation period. By way of illustration, the

30

output of one large clandestine documentation center in
south eastern France, financed in part by contributions
from an American Jewish organization, for the month of
March 1944 was as follows: 1895 identity cards, 1300 work
permissions, 1250 birth certificates, 428 demobilization
cards, 920 baptismal certificates, 124 ration cards, 27
naturalization certificates, 25 marriage certificates and
1500 "lavages," that is, the chemical removal of names,
dates and the like.

One of the most heart-rending tasks in France under
the Nazis and Laval was the protection of Jewish children
from deportation. This work was carried on by a number of
organizations but with particular success and courage by
the Union O.S.E. ("Oeuvre de Secours aux Enfants") which,
in May 1945, had close to 5000 Jewish children under its
charge, part of them abandoned, part of them in hiding with
their parents. About 250 new ones had to be taken in each
month. The OSE's technique, which was typical of all such
work, consisted in falsifying the child's identity, changing
its residence and placing it in a non-Jewish private family
or institution. With the intensification of the Allied
bombing offensive during the spring of 1945 the OSE had
good success with placing such children in colonies set up
for French children evacuated from heavily bombed regions.
The amount of contact work involved in carrying out this
program was enormous, of course, and the danger of constant
travel by social workers, most of them Jewish, great and
ever-present. Extraordinary precautions had to be taken to
avoid the concentration of too many children in any given
area; but even so the OSE's office in Geneva frequently
received those tragic messages telling of the sudden and
brutal arrest by the Gestapo of a small group of children,
along with one or two faithful social workers, and their
transport to Drancy, the notorious Nazi deportation center
for Jews, located on the outskirts of Paris.

31

Such "protective" work in behalf of endangered Jews in France, both children and adults, was in general adequately financed from Switzerland by such large Jewish organizations as the JDC. The Board in Switzerland, therefore, directed its aid into less well supplied channels. Accordingly in June 1944 a major contribution from WRB discretionary funds went to the Social Service Section of the central French resistance movement, the C.N.R. or "Conseil National de la Résistance," primarily to assist the French in shouldering the terrible and ever increasing burden of aid to the families of men tortured, executed and deported by the Germans. Our grant was in turn split up by the C.N.R. among a number of agencies, political, confessional and occupational, specializing in different types of aid: parcels to men and women in the prisons, direct financial subsidies to women and children whose breadwinner was gone, social welfare work, maintenance for persons in hiding, the production and distribution of false documents and, occasionally, the organization of prison breaks.* A sum of half a million French francs, for instance, went to Father Godard, director of the special relief service of Cardinal Gerlier in Lyon. This sum was instrumental in organizing the release of some 200 wounded "maquisards" held prisoners by the Gestapo in the hospital of Antiquaille in Lyon awaiting their sufficient recovery so they could be executed! Such Board aid to the French resistance movement also served the purpose of enlisting the help and cooperation of the French underground in favor of foreigners on French soil, in danger of their lives for either racial or political reasons.

Smaller grants from WRB funds were also made directly for the relief of such foreign groups in France: specifically the Spaniards and the refugee Germans. The former, numbering

---

* For complete details see pages 8, 9 and 10 of WRB, Bern financial report of November 27, 1944.

many tens of thousands, had been living a precarious and
wretched existence mostly in south western France since 1939
when they fled from Spain at the time of the collapse of
the Spanish Republic. Yet this did not prevent many of them
from taking a courageous and active part in the general
armed resistance against the Nazis and in the wide-spread
campaign of sabotage of the German army communication system
in France. But when a Spaniard went down fighting or was
executed by the Gestapo there was really no agency with adequate means to which his family could legitimately turn for
aid.

The lot of the German or Austrian political refugee
(or for that matter of the Italian, Yugoslav or Greek) who
in most cases had spent a year or more in a Nazi concentration camp or prison was even more bleak in France. To make
matters worse a great many Spaniards and Germans, particularly if they were Jews, were suffering further privation in
the notoriously bad refugee internment camps and foreign
workers' companies of the Vichy government from whence many
of the so-called "politicals" were once more turned over to
their Nazi oppressors. This happened to the majority of the
internees in the camp of Le Vernet in the department of the
Ariège, for example. Or if they were not redeported by the
Germans Vichy shipped them to its forced labor bataillons
in the North African wastes.

Through its representative in Switzerland financial
contributions were made by the Board both for the aid of
the Spaniards (in May and August 1944) and of the German
political refugees (in July 1944). Our assistance to the
latter group went through the Unitarian Service Committee
whose office in Switzerland maintained close contact with
the main organization of German political refugees in France.
This aid was used principally to support persons in hiding
and to finance the sending of food parcels into prisons and
camps.

WRB financial grants to the Spaniards in France

were channelled through the representative of their "Comité
d'Union National" in Geneva and served a double purpose.
Besides helping them organize more and better relief for
their own people in France this money enlisted the invaluable
aid of the Spanish partisan units operating in the chain of
the Pyrenées from Cerbère to Hendaye in passing Jewish refugees into Spain. This escape route was dangerous and
difficult and involved ten to fifteen hours on foot through
mountainous country so that it was open only to the most
robust. The number of individuals who got out to safety this
way was therefore comparatively small. Estimates vary
according to the organization consulted, but between 700 and
a 1000 endangered persons must have escaped by this route.
Two or three Jewish organizations operating in Switzerland,
notably the JDC and the World Jewish Congress, financed the
"French end" of this work (whereas part of our WRB contribution had gone into Spain), that is the transport and
assembling of the refugees in a suitable place of departure
generally located in the Tarbes region of the department of
the Basses Pyrenées.

In the interest of/both obtaining more aid for the
Spaniards and increasing the effectiveness of this rescue
work over the mountains into Spain, the Board's representative
was able to establish the necessary contact between other
Jewish committees in Switzerland and the Spanish C.U.N. In
June 1944, for instance, the representative in Switzerland
of the Union of Orthodox Rabbis of the United States made
a sum of 100,000 Swiss francs available to Dr. Weil of the
Union OSE which was used almost exclusively, part of it
going to the Spaniards, to further this work.

In connection with France the WRB office in Bern was
also able to assist in a variety of ways with the passing
of Jewish children over into Switzerland, although the increasing difficulty of bringing children up to the border on
the French side, during the spring of 1944, precluded any

large-scale rescue action along these lines. The Board's
representative had frequent conversations with the chief of
the Swiss Federal Police as well as informal talks with the
officers of the military police charged with border surveillance in the Geneva area. In March 1944 when authorization for 4000 United States immigration visas for children
from France reached Switzerland the occasion was taken to
formally impress upon the Government of Switzerland the
United States Government's earnest hope "that such action,
direct and indirect, as will facilitate and expedite the
movement of children into Switzerland from France" would be
taken. As a matter of fact in December 1943 the Federal
Police had already signified Switzerland's willingness to
admit an initial contingent of 1500 Jewish children (boys
up to 16 years of age and girls up to 18) through such
clandestine channels as a result of representations made in
Bern by a group of private refugee relief agencies. This
quota, unfortunately, was never reached due rather to the
aforementioned difficulty of getting the children up to the
border in France (disrupted communications and the growing
unrest in the Haute Savoie and Jura regions which broke into
open insurrection shortly after the Normandy landings in
June 1944) rather than to any lack of cooperation on the
part of the Swiss authorities. Between January and July 1944
barely 600 abandoned refugee children were brought over; and
about again as many reached Switzerland in the company of their
parents or relatives.

  With respect to adults fleeing from France to Switzerland an unofficial arrangement was made with the Swiss
police by the Board's representative, in collaboration with
the members of other relief agencies, whereby the names of
particularly endangered individuals waiting in France to
cross the border could be submitted and advance consent for
their entry obtained.

  In reply to much sharp criticism levelled by various

35

organizations and persons against the Swiss police on the
subject of turning fugitives back at the frontier it must
in all fairness be pointed out that the equitable application
of border control measures at a time when thousands of individuals, many not at all in danger of their lives and often
undesirables, were attempting to enter Switzerland illegally,
were extraordinarily difficult. Inevitably isolated refugees
were turned back who should perhaps have been admitted. The
overall percentage of those granted asylum, however, in relation to the number who presented themselves at the frontiers
was over ninety-five according to the actual statistical
records.

The WRB was further able to facilitate the movement
of persecuted persons from France into Switzerland by small
financial contributions to such local organizations as the
"Franc-Tireur Partisan" group in the Haute Savoie which
"occupied" a considerable stretch of the Franco-Swiss border
outside Geneva. As customary in the case of grants to
underground organizations it was our understanding that part
of our help should be used for the legitimate relief activities of the F.T.P. themselves. Or again a modest monthly
sum given to a Dutch committee in Geneva which had established
a fortunate contact assured the cooperation of a minor Swiss
official in the military reception camp in Geneva where incoming refugees were "screened" prior to being definitely
admitted or sent back. His help consisted mainly in holding
special cases longer than the usual three days until adequate intercession could be taken in Bern, since the border
police were often in too much of a hurry, particularly when
there was a large influx, to "refouler" the doubtful cases.

Finally, for the further relief of persecuted persons
in France, the Board's office in Switzerland financed three
small shipments, which went in through clandestine channels,
of medicines, sanitary equipment and pharmaceuticals. These
supplies crossed the border in May, June and August 1944.

In all these activities it must not be forgotten that

36

such aid rendered by an American organization to France,
whether in response to the dire need of the French resistance or to succour persecuted foreign groups, had a value
far above its intrinsic one in that it strengthened the will
to resist of thousands of sorely tried men and women and
made them feel that they were not entirely abandoned in
their bitter struggle against great odds.

HUNGARY

On March 19, 1944, a few weeks after the creation
of the War Refugee Board in the United States and shortly
before the setting-up of Board representation at the
American Legation in Bern, Switzerland, Nazi forces moved
into Hungary. This last armed German penetration of a
major European country, one, to be sure, which was already
an ally of the Third Reich, preluded one of the most
ruthless operations in the long and infamous Nazi campaign
of persecution against a Jewish minority. With the willing
and cruel assistance of a well-established anti-semitic
faction in Hungary itself, Himmler's SS organization
succeeded, in the short space of eight months, in decimating
a Jewish community of almost 800,000 souls so that today
after the Germans have been driven out scarcely 150,000
survivors remain in Hungary proper. Between mid-April
and the end of June 1944 alone over 300,000 Hungarian Jews
were deported from the provinces, particularly of north-
eastern Hungary and Carpatho-Russia, to death for the majority of them, in the camps of Upper Silesia.

The intensity and brutality of this attack on so
large a number of defenseless men, women and children immediately enlisted in countermeasure all the energy and
resources of the newly formed War Refugee Board. A great
deal of the action taken by the Board passed through Bern

37

the point located, strategically speaking, as close to
Hungary as it was possible for an American mission to be
at that time.

The tragic account of the Nazi-satellite assault
on the Jews in Hungary, in all its bitter and heart-rending
complexity, would fill the pages of a considerable volume.
An attempt will be made, therefore, to touch upon only the
high points of the WRB's action, as carried on through
Switzerland, in an effort to forestall, mitigate or halt
this frightful wave of persecution which swept over Hungary
in the late spring, summer and fall of 1944.

The methods used to aid the Jews in Hungary as
effectively as possible and the channels of approach to
this dreadful problem exploited are essentially those
which were employed in all Board action in Europe, the
choice of method being varied or the stress shifted according
to the particular circumstances. These lines of attack may
be generally defined as the following: politico-diplomatic,
financial and propaganda. The secondary services of
liaison and information formed an integral part of the above
three. In the case of Hungary the principal technique can
best be termed that of "preventative pressure" exercised
through diplomatic channels and by means of propaganda
measures. Direct assistance in the form of financial grants
was also given and constituted a valuable tool.

As soon as it became unmistakably evident toward the
end of May that the Hungarian Jews were being deported "en
masse" and under the most barbarous conditions the most urgent
task was that of attempting to bring the Hungarian government
and people to their senses by means of formal warnings
transmitted by the competent services of the Legation through
the Swiss government. A first strong message was despatched
from Bern early in June and delivered by the Swiss minister
in Budapest to the Hungarian Foreign Office. An immediate
explanation of acts which were shocking the entire civilized
world was demanded and the Hungarians were reminded in

unequivocal terms that it was the determination of the
Government of the United States, as set forth in President
Roosevelt's declaration of March 24, 1944, on the murder of
innocent civilians by the enemy, "to see to it that all
those who share in the guilt (of such acts) shall share the
punishment."

During the ensuing months, in both formal notes and
in conversations with the American Minister at Bern, the
Swiss authorities were reminded of the great concern of
our Government and people that no step be left untaken
to bring all possible aid to such victims of persecution.
The Swiss were urged to do their utmost to render whatever
assistance possible through all channels open to them.
As a result their mission in Budapest was helpful in a
number of ways: 1) the issuance of protective documents to
holders of Palestine certificates (during July Mr. Krausz,
the representative of the Jewish Agency for Palestine,
was permitted to open an office on the premises of the
Swiss Legation), 2) the granting of all possible protection
with a view to preserving them from deportation or at least
exempting them from forced labor service to persons possessing the documentation of Latin-American countries whose
interests the Swiss represented in Hungary, 3) numerous
approaches to both the German and Hungarian authorities in
an effort to obtain exit permissions and facilities for
those categories of Jews recognized as emigrable by both
the Germans and Hungarians at the end of July 1944, and
finally 4) many individual acts of courage and devotion performed by individual members of the Swiss mission in behalf
of the persecuted Jews in Hungary.

On July 14, 1944 the Swiss Federal Political Department in Bern informed the American Legation that instructions
had been given the Swiss Minister at Budapest "to leave no
doubt in the mind of the Hungarian government with regard to
the attitude of the Swiss government and the Swiss people

39

concerning these persecutions and to make it clear ...
that the good relations and the high regard which the Swiss
government and people had for Hungary would undoubtedly be
adversely effected by a continuance of this policy." The
Swiss Foreign Minister, M. Pilet-Golaz, spoke to the Hungarian Minister in Bern in the same terms.

During July the Swiss Federal Council also signified
its willingness to admit to temporary asylum in Switzerland
some 5000 Jewish children and expectant mothers from Hungary;
and again in August declared that Switzerland would receive
on its territory, pending their transport, elsewhere, from
7 to 8000 holders of Palestine entry certificates if these
refugees could not leave Hungary to the eastward. A few
days later the Swiss authorities agreed to expand this agreement to include the right of transit and temporary sojourn
of some 4500 possessors of Swedish protective documents from
Budapest who could not proceed directly to Sweden.

In the field of less formal political intercession,
not long after the setting up of the War Refugee Board in
Washington, the Board's appointee in Switzerland sent a
preliminary "feeler" on March 9, 1944 through the Hungarian
minister in Bern to the Hungarian government. In view of
the role which Hungary had hitherto played, due largely to
its geographic location, as an asylum for Jewish refugees
fleeing from persecution in Poland and Slovakia, the Hungarian
government was queried as to the extent it would be willing
"to develop or assist in the development of programs and
the implementation of measures for the rescue, transportation
and maintenance of refugees and victims of persecution -
racial, religious or political - who were in imminent danger
of death." Again on May 6th. the by that time ex-Hungarian
minister at Bern, Baron Bakach-Bessenyey, was informally
persuaded to despatch a message through the Hungarian Legation
addressed to the Hungarian Foreign Office in which the
attention of the government was drawn to the importance of
the recently created War Refugee Board (with special stress

on President Roosevelt's interest in it) and particularly
to the Board 's aim of mitigating discriminatory measures
against innocent racial minorities. It was suggested that
it would be good policy to allow the Jews in Hungary to
receive aid in both money and kind from recognized relief
agencies, both indigenous and international (such as the
International Red Cross) and to permit the emigration of
various categories of Jews who could leave Hungary,
especially children. At the close of this note the very
obvious efforts being made by the rival Rumanian government
to atone for its former anti-semitic policy were underlined.

The Board's representative in Switzerland undertook
similar informal approaches early in June to the Rumanian
minister in Bern, M. Vespiamu Pella, as well as to the delegate of the Rumanian Red Cross in Geneva, M. Suneriu, in
an effort to obtain more lenient entry and transit rights
into Rumania for Jews fleeing persecution in Hungary. Conversations were also held with M. De Koever, the representative of the Hungarian Red Cross in Switzerland, with the
purpose of warning certain circles in Hungary, particularly
those close to Imredy, with whom De Koever was known to be
in personal touch, to mend their evil ways with regard to
this question of Jewish persecution if they had any hopes
for their personal futures. At this time De Koever was also
supplied with a copy of the Board's informal message of
May 6th, which had been transmitted by Baron Bakach-Bessenyey
and which set forth the specific concessions for the Jews
desired by the American Government and the War Refugee Board.

Throughout the anguished months of the attack on the
Jewish minority in Hungary the Board in Switzerland was also
in constant contact with the International Committee of the
Red Cross in Geneva. No doubt was left in the minds of the
leading members of the Committee as to the attitude of the
United States Government or of its expectancy that the Red
Cross would do all in its power to undertake effective action
in behalf of these persecuted people. At the outset of the

41

anti-Jewish measures in Hungary the ICRC was requested, on March 28, 1944, to increase the size and strength of its representation in this country "in order to protect the well-being of groups ... who are facing persecution." Although it was not immediately possible for the Committee to send in additional delegates, mainly due to the difficulty of obtaining the necessary German transit visas, its President, Dr. Max Huber, gave assurance that the Committee was working on this problem and some weeks later framed and sent a strong personal letter addressed to Admiral Horthy which undoubtedly contributed to the suspension of the deportation of the Jews from Hungary early in July 1944. Later in this month the ICRC was able to transfer one of their most capable delegates from Germany, Dr. Schirmer, to Budapest where, in cooperation with Mr. Born, he inaugurated a very helpful program of food relief for the over-crowded Jewish quarters, set up special children's homes under the insignia of the International Committee, and undertook considerable protective action in favor of the personnel and property of the local Jewish relief agencies. These ICRC programs continued successfully until the Soviet forces took Budapest early in 1945. During the short-lived Szalasi-Arrow-Cross régime the energetic personal intercession of the members of the ICRC's mission undoubtedly saved the lives of a great many Hungarian Jews.

In addition to promoting action through the Swiss Government and the International Committee of the Red Cross the representative of the WRB kept closely in touch with church groups in Switzerland whose leaders were regularly supplied with detailed information concerning the inhuman persecution of the Jews going on in Hungary and urged to appeal through their congregations and government that appropriate Swiss countermeasures be taken. Thus the Swiss Protestant churches, through the energetic spokesmanship of the director of their refugee service, Pastor Paul Vogt, submitted a strong plea in June for preventative action to the President of the Confederation. Similar messages including financial aid (received under special license from Protestant groups in the United States) were sent to the fairly _influential_ Hungarian Reformed Church group which played a courageous, if limited, role in assisting the persecuted Jewish minority and in bringing pressure to bear on the Hungarian government. Numerous talks were also had with the Papal Nuncio in Bern, Monsignor Bernardini, and with persons close to Monsignor Besson, the highest Catholic dignitary in Switzerland, who likewise made known to the Federal Council the hopes of the Catholic population of Switzerland that their government would do all in its power to allieviate the suffering of the Jews in Hungary.

Contacts for the same purpose were established and fostered with other leaders of Swiss public opinion, particularly political, such as Dr. Hans Oprecht, the leader of the Swiss Socialist Party and with the Secretary General of the Swiss Workers' Party (the Communists), Karl Hofmeier, in order that these men might in turn enlist the support of their parties in Switzerland and elsewhere in the interest of the Hungarian Jews.

Perhaps best described as political steps of an even less orthodox nature were the difficult "negotiations" with the SS in Hungary carried on in and from Switzerland in a long-drawn out and tortuous effort to obtain concessions for the Jews still alive in Hungary and later for other categories of equally defenseless and innocent civil detainees in German hands. The burden of these negotiations was courageously and adroitly born by Mr. Saly Mayer, who negotiated as a Swiss citizen and as president of the Swiss Jewish Relief Fund, although he was also the representative in Switzerland of the American Jewish Joint Distribution Committee. From the outset the Board's representative in Bern, without directly participating in the numerous discussions pertaining to this affair except on one special occasion, gave all possible

43

support and backing to Mr. Mayer's efforts.

Begun in Hungary and Istamboul in May of 1944 by members of the Budapest Jewish Community in a desperate attempt to deter the Nazis from their fast-moving and diabolic plan to eliminate Hungarian Jewry, these negotiations shifted to Switzerland in July when it became apparent that it would not be possible for the European director of the JDC, an American citizen, to conduct them himself. At the request of the WRB the representative of the Board in Switzerland kept Washington constantly informed on the progress of this action. In order to facilitate Mr. Mayer's trying task rapid and secure communication services through the Legation were made available to him and the Board was later instrumental in securing special U.S. Treasury licenses to permit the JDC in America to transmit funds to strengthen Mr. Mayer's hand as a negotiator. The Board's representative had frequent conversations with the Swiss authorities in the interest of enrolling their aid and interpreting to them the concern of the American Government that such efforts whose purpose was in the last analysis humanitarian go forward. Specific intervention was made with the Swiss Federal Police regarding the granting of necessary entry permits for the German negotiators during November 1944, as well as to explain the need of the numerous meetings which Mr. Mayer had to arrange on the Swiss border.

The primary purpose of these negotiations which were conducted with the SS commercial representative for Hungary, "Obersturmbannführer" Kurt Becher, was to gain time and meanwhile obtain surcease in the deportation measures against the Hungarian Jews. The technique employed, of which Mr. Mayer was a master, consisted in talking: promising, cajoling, intimating, threatening - in short keeping a continual series of proposals and counter-proposals going. In this delicate task Mr. Mayer was ably seconded by a leading Budapest

Zionist and lawyer, Dr. Isreal Kasztner, who acted with
courage and resourcefulness for over a year as interme-
diary between Becher of the SS and Mr. Mayer. Dealing
with the Nazis in this specific problem was considerably
facilitated by the rivalry existing between factions within
the ranks of the SS and the resulting "jockeying" for
prestige and success. Early in the German action against
the Jews in Hungary contact was established by Dr. Kasztner
with the commercial wing of the SS under Becher and the
idea planted that there might be certain material advantages,
if not personal at least for the SS, to be derived in not
eliminating the Jews in so rapid and ruthless a manner.
In order that discussions along these lines could be taken
up, however, it would be absolutely necessary to check the
barbaric activities of the SS "Special Commando," headed by
the notorious SS "Obersturmbannführer" Karl Eichmann, charged
with deporting the Jews from Hungary. The suggestion appealed
to Becher who was already beginning to enjoy the role of
"gentleman-administrator" over the "leased" Manfred-Weiss
industrial concerns which had fallen to him. Although an
ardent Nazi Becher liked to think of himself as a soldier
and a gentleman who did not descend to the murderer's trade
plied by Eichmann and his henchmen, Hunsche and Wisliceny.
On the other hand Becher was very interested in cutting a
successful figure in the eyes of his "chief," Himmler
with whom his relations were more direct and cordial than
Eichmann's. This meant obtaining results of a commercial
value to the SS. Throughout, therefore, a long series of
meetings, generally at St. Margarethen on the Swiss-Austrian
frontier, which began in August of 1944 and continued periodically until as late as April 1945 and were conducted with
astuteness and skill by Mr. Mayer, Becher and his various
colleagues (Krumey, Kettlitz, Gruson and Krell) were led to
believe that eventually they would secure if not commercial
at least monetary concessions of considerable value if they

45

succeeded, in opposition to Eichmann, in sufficiently
mitigating the lot of the Hungarian Jews in particular
and that of other Jews and civil detainees in general, in
Europe. Every imaginable dilatory tactic was employed;
and yet the delicate balance between going too far and
not offering enough and dangling goods and money before
Becher's eyes was always somehow maintained. Meanwhile
there were always breaches of good faith (the general
agreement having been that while negotiations went on all
deportation of Jews should be halted) on the part of the
SS - the attack on the Jews in Slovakia in September 1944,
for instance, or the forced evacuation on foot of several
thousand Hungarian Jews from Budapest in November 1944 -
which afforded Mr. Mayer an excuse to threaten to break
off the discussions and to dampen the Nazis' hurry to obtain material advantages. And as Germany's military situation
grew worse Becher and his men, feeling less and less secure,
tended to demand less and in the last analysis to hope
(although they never openly admitted this) that in these
continued discussions and concessions granted they might
save their own skins.

In retrospect it is difficult to understand how
these negotiations could have been prolonged to this extent
with no actual goods or money having ever been given yet
so much, relatively speaking, gained when more than once
we thought that the game was up and that the Nazis had
lost patience.

Aside from regularly securing a great deal of
invaluable first-hand information from Dr. Kasztner concerning the progress and plans of the Nazi-Hungarian operations
against the Jews, the tangible results of these negotiations
can be summed up as the following:

1) The bringing to Switzerland of the two groups of
Jews from Hungary, via the concentration camp of Bergen-
Belsen, on August 21, 1944 (318 persons) and on December
6, 1944 (1355 persons).

2) The avoidance of the deportation of upwards of 200,000 Jews remaining in Budapest on August 25, 1944 when Eichmann's organization had 66 trains ready.

3) The exemption, as far as the Germans were concerned (the excesses which occurred being due almost exclusively to the cruelty of the Arrow-Cross thugs who were out to liquidate the Jews whereas the Germans were interested in labor), of elderly and sick persons and children (Becher's orders had been no one under 16, no women over 40 or men over 60) from the forced evacuation on foot of Jews from Budapest in November 1944.

4) The diverting of transports of some 17,000 Hungarian Jews to Austria rather than to Auschwitz in June 1944. At least 80% of these persons were reported still in Austria at the time of the Soviet occupation.

5) Tacit SS agreement that the International Committee of the Red Cross be permitted in Budapest and environs to shelter some 3000 Jewish children in homes under the Committee's protection. (August through December 1944)

6) Facilities for the procurement and distribution of foodstuffs and clothing to some 7000 Jews in labor camps in the Vienna region (January 1945).

7) The release and arrival in Switzerland of 69 prominent Jews formerly from Slovakia and Hungary on April 18, 1945.

Although this cannot be definitely listed as a result obtained Becher claimed during his last conversations with Mr. Mayer in April 1945 that he, Becher, had been instrumental in "neutralizing" and arranging the surrender of the camp of Bergen-Belsen to the advancing British forces. Kasztner was there with him at that time. It has, however, never been possible to substantiate this or to determine how great a service this constituted if actually performed by Becher.

It cannot, of course, be claimed that Mr. Mayer's negotiations with Becher were exclusively and solely responsible for the above-mentioned results. Yet they un-

47

doubtedly contributed in very large measure to their
attainment.

The second important general method through which
the Board could initiate helpful action from Switzerland
was the financial. The sending in of money to support
rescue and relief operations being carried on by responsible
agencies in Hungary (as well as in other neighboring countries
such as Slovakia, Rumania and Austria) constituted one of
the most flexible and useful means of rendering rapid aid.
Such financial assistance was of two types: direct and
indirect. By the former, out and out contributions from
WRB discretionary funds are meant; the second refers to
the extensive system of special U. S. Treasury licenses
which the Board sponsored so that reliable relief organizations
could receive adequate contributions from their supporters
in the United States which in turn could be employed to
finance their rescue programs in enemy and enemy-occupied
areas. Prior to the inauguration of the WRB's intensive
program in behalf of persecuted and endangered persons in
Axis-controlled territory the regulations of the Allied
economic blockade had prohibited the remittance of funds
for use in enemy controlled areas. In reversing this
procedure on a limited and controlled scale in deference to
the desperate plight of tens of thousands of innocent men,
women and children suffering persecution naturally every
precaution was taken that such funds transmitted to Budapest, Bratislava, Bucharest or Vienna, as the case might be,
should in no way aid the Axis. In the overwhelming majority
of the transactions supervized by the Board's representative
in Switzerland there is no evidence that the enemy derived
any benefit whatever from funds thus sent into territory
under his control; and a valuable weapon was placed in the
hands of the relief agencies to combat the enemy's evil
designs.

In the cases of Hungary, Slovakia, Rumania and
Austria the principal private relief agency financing rescue

operations was the American Jewish Joint Distribution
Committee which, through their representative in Switzerland, Mr. Saly Mayer, regularly transferred money into the
above-mentioned countries. Smaller and less regular
remittances were made by such other agencies as the Union
of Orthodox Rabbis of the United States into the same
countries generally for the relief of some specific group.
Such money served to cover in the first place the unprecedented need for relief resulting from the drastic measures
of economic discrimination which had rapidly reduced the
Jewish minorities to the state of paupers. It also served
the many emergency rescue measures taken by the local
organizations to save their people from deportation.

In addition to cash remittances (or the releasing of
local currency by clearing operations) to Budapest for
the Jews in Hungary, the JDC, through Mr. Mayer, financed
the purchase of food supplies in Rumania and the procurement of specialized supplies such as medicines and condensed
milk in Switzerland for Hungary. Steamer passages to
Palestine via Turkey for Jewish refugees in Rumania, many
of whom came from Hungary, were paid for through Switzerland by the "Joint". This was an action which had a most
important if indirect bearing on the rescue of Jews in
Hungary, hundreds of whom were escaping over the border into
Rumania. In the interest of keeping this flow going and
preserving the continued acquiescence of the Antonescu
government it was imperative that steps be taken to
evacuate as many such fugitives as possible from Rumania.

Several considerable direct grants from WRB discretionary funds were made from its office in Switzerland
for aid to the persecuted Jews in the Balkans through the
small but well-organized young Jewish people's organization,
the Hechaluz, whose groups were very active in Hungary,
Slovakia and Rumania in rescue and related activities. Such
Board contributions covered the manifold expenses involved
in emergency, illegal rescue work: the maintenance of persons

49

in hiding, the purchase, acquisition or fabrication of ration cards, travel permits, birth, baptismal and "aryan" certificates, the buying of foodstuffs, clothing, medicines, the payment of train and other transportation costs, the covering of the overhead of frequently moved offices and headquarters, the maintenance of personnel in the field, and the enlisting of the aid or acquiescence of minor officials, peasants, and border guards.

WRB funds were also used in Switzerland to defray the costs of a courier service to Budapest, Bratislava and Bucharest (including, occasionally, Prague and Vienna) so that vital communications might be kept open during those many critical months. Another small Board "grant" went to enroll the aid of the clandestine Communist press in Switzerland and adjoining territories.

50

Because of the geographical location of Hungary and since it was in generally too unwieldy a relief tool, the Board office in Switzerland, with the exception of one restricted shipment of medical supplies into northern Yugoslavia via partisan channels for Jewish refugees who had escaped from southern Hungary, did not purchase and send in relief goods. Such work was more practically left to the competent services of the local relief agencies in Hungary itself or in neighboring food producing areas such as Rumania.

As a further contribution to the financial side of assistance to persecuted persons in the Balkans it was occasionally possible for the Board's representative in Bern, as a result of the many people seen and contacts maintained, to advise relief agencies of advantageous possibilities or arrangements for the acquisition of local currency in various countries of south-eastern Europe. This was usually done through private clearing schemes where an individual or concern in Switzerland was willing to release funds in Budapest or elsewhere against Swiss francs deposited in Switzerland.

In this connection as well as with respect to many
other matters within the scope of the Board's activity,
mainly of an informational nature, the WRB office at the
American Legation in Bern could render valuable assistance
as a liaison agency. The programs or plans of separate
individuals or committees working independently could frequently be coordinated. Often they could be given the
benefit of the latest information regarding a special
situation whether it was the passing of children from France
to Switzerland or the most reliable means of communicating
with northern Italy. At all times during the period of
WRB activity in Switzerland a great deal of personal interviewing was carried on although our main effort was focused on
the larger task of organizing, stimulating and supporting
wider relief and rescue programs. It was nevertheless
impossible to turn away the distraught individuals whose
loved-ones were caught up in the maelstrom of Nazi persecution
in a dozen European countries. They had to be comforted,
advised and guided to whatever organization or individual
might have some chance of helping them with their particular
problem.

       51

In the field of liaison work the WRB in Bern made
a point of keeping in close touch with the representatives
in Switzerland of the various European resistance movements
through whom it was often possible to initiate helpful action
in favor of endangered persons or minorities in enemy-occupied
regions. Cases in point are the Board's financial aid to
the underground in Slovakia, given through the Czech representative in Geneva, by means of which military action by
partisan forces was undertaken which resulted in the liberation of the concentration camps for Jews of Novaky and
Sered in August of 1944 at the time of the general uprising
against the Nazis, and the freeing of close to 1500 detainees;
or again our contribution to the northern Italian G.A.P.
groups ("Gruppi d'Azione Patriotici") which helped to finance
a number of prison breaks for patriots condemned to death or

deportation.

In searching for usable ways and means of combatting the campaign of persecution undertaken in Hungary, a region which was not directly accessible to Switzerland, the psychological weapon of propaganda could not be neglected. With the help of a capable research assistant the collection of authentic documentary material from all available sources (private correspondence and reports, Hungarian and German radios and particularly the Hungarian press) concerning the anti-Jewish measures was immediately undertaken. This information was periodically issued during June and July 1944 in the form of mimeographed bulletins which appeared in French, German and English. These were made available to selected Swiss newspaper editors, influential political figures in Switzerland, church groups and any other organization or individual in a position to reach or influence a block of Swiss public opinion. The result was considerable space in the Swiss press concerning happenings which would probably otherwise have been passed over with a line or two and would not have created much more of an impression on the Swiss public than what had sceptically come to be known as "horror propaganda" normally did. All official statements from the United States such as the President's declaration of March 24, 1944, Archbishop Spellman's statement and Governor Dewey's and Secretary Hull's pronouncements on the subject of persecution in enemy territory which were naturally released to the larger Swiss press by the Bern branch of the Office of War Information were also made available by the Board's representative to the clandestine press in Hungary, northern Italy, Czechoslovakia, Austria, France and even Switzerland (Communist newspapers). It was later gratifying to note that the Germans in Hungary had been forced to take into account the complaints of the Hungarian government concerning "foreign press attacks." This was not without effect in compelling the Sztojay-Horthy government to back down regarding the

further deportation of Jews from Hungary. The Hungarians
were particularly vulnerable to the accusation of practicing
mass cruelty and intolerance since up to the very last
they hypocritically vaunted themselves as a "Kulturstaat"
preserving in the midst of a rapidly bolchevized Europe
the ancient and Christian traditions of the Crown of Saint
Stephan.

Naturally at all times the high points of such information concerning the latest developments in the situation
in Hungary were transmitted to the Board in Washington, so
that as the WRB deemed useful it could be made available to
the larger apparatus of official Allied psychological
warfare.

RUMANIA

Aside from the informal diplomatic approaches to
the Rumanian Minister in Bern and to the delegate of the
Rumanian Red Cross in Geneva previously mentioned, the
Board's representative in Switzerland undertook little
direct action in Rumania in connection with the persecution
of the Jews in the Balkans. A portion of our WRB financial
grants were used in this country by the Hechaluz for the
maintenance of relay stations just off the Hungarian border
for fugitives arriving in Rumania and funds were sent to
Bucharest and to Istamboul for the financing of the steamer
transport of Jewish refugees in Rumania to Palestine by the
Joint Distribution Committee. In relation, however, to
the particular question of steamers and sea transportation
for Jewish refugees leaving such Rumanian ports as Constanza
the International Committee of the Red Cross was very
active. The importance of the Committee's contribution to
this task which dated back as far as 1942 must not be
underestimated. From March of that year up to the time of
the Russian occupation of Rumania the ICRC repeatedly

and in part to a "negotiated" modus vivendi with the SS.
Too, the Tiso government and its Hlinka guard were never
as zealous in their anti-semitic program as their Hungarian
counterparts. Indeed between April and September 1944
many hundreds of Jews fled from Hungary to Slovakia, particularly Bratislava, in order to escape deportation. Among
them, ironically enough, were persons who had previously
sought asylum in Hungary during 1942 when mass deportations of Jews from Slovakian territory to Upper Silesia
had taken place.

Board action in Slovakia and the aid sent in by
such private agencies of the "Joint" and the Union of
Orthodox Rabbis during the spring and summer of 1944
was on a small scale in comparison to that despatched to
Hungary and limited to financial help. Funds were transmitted fairly regularly to finance the flight of Jews
from Hungary (and to a small extent, alas, from Poland)
and particularly to cover the costs of the maintenance of
several thousands of refugees clandestinely in Slovakia.

In September 1944, as a result of the armed uprising
of the partisan groups in Slovakia, the situation of the
Jews there became more critical since a certain number of
their younger people had taken an active and understandable
part in this insurrection.* Accordingly more active and
extensive countermeasures on the part of the Board office
in Switzerland were rapidly planned and undertaken. Financial contributions were stepped up and efforts were made,
through the Papal Nuncio and the Vatican, to bring special
pressure to bear on the Tiso government by means of warnings
similar to those delivered to the Hungarian government. In
spite of these steps and because the Germans could invoke
the excuse of "military necessity," between 3 and 4000
Jews were brutally rounded up in Bratislava by the SS with

55

* In the course of conversations with Becher of the SS about
  a month after this uprising, the latter reproached Saly
  Mayer for the role the young Jews had played in the resistance. Saly asked him if he, Becher, could conscien-
  tiously expect a young Jew to join the SS!

the assistance of the Hlinka Guard on the night of September 28 to 29, 1944, concentrated in the assembly camp of Sered and deported shortly thereafter to Poland. A parallel action was conducted in the provinces still under German control and many Jews were shot or killed on the spot.

Diplomatic action through the Swiss government in the case of Slovakia was difficult because the United States had never recognized the Tiso "government" and the Swiss themselves only maintained de facto consular representation in Bratislava. The American Legation in Bern, however, requested the Swiss government to lodge a strong protest with the German authorities for the removal from Slovakia of some 360 Jews holding Latin-American documentation (principally Salvadoran and Paraguayan) or claiming other western hemisphere nationalities including that of the United States who had also been deported from Sered and from a special camp at Marianka outside Bratislava. This intercession was repeated in February 1945 after it had been possible to acquire a list of these persons and attained some limited success in that about thirteen individuals claiming United States citizenship were finally returned. No news was ever obtained concerning the whereabouts of the others although the information was received that the SS had simply torn up their Latin-American nationality certificates claiming that they were false.

It was also unfortunately not possible to take effective steps in Slovakia during the crisis period through the International Red Cross since the latter was unable to get a delegate into Bratislava until the end of October. There is good evidence that the Gestapo purposely withheld granting the necessary transit visa until their operation against the Jews in September and early October was carried through. This fact is characteristic of the inadequacy of the weapons which we could bring to bear

in comparison to those normally available to the Germans.
When M. Dunand, the ICRC representative, finally did
reach Bratislava in late October he interceded energetically
on a number of occasions throughout the month of November
in behalf of more liberal treatment for the Jews remaining
in the camp at Sered (although permission to visit this
camp was never granted to him by the German police) and for
the handfull still at Marianka. Dunand made several representations to the local Slovak authorities including
the commander of the Hlinka Guard (then chief of the Slovak
police) and although they displayed a noticeable disposition
to be less severe in their handling of the Jews than the
SS little was obtainable in the face of a general German
order to the effect that all Slovak Jews should be transported to German territory "for the duration of the war."*
The continued presence of an ICRC delegate in Bratislava
did, however, greatly facilitate relief action for the many
other Jews of both Slovak and other nationalities who were
in hiding there. Through him it was possible for the Jewish
organizations in Switzerland, particularly the JDC, to
transmit funds with greater assurance that they would reach
their intended beneficiaries.

57

About the only contact possible from Switzerland with
Poland was maintained over Bratislava; and it was through
this city that a part of the relief supplies purchased by
the International Red Cross with funds supplied, at the
instigation of the War Refugee Board, by the Joint Distribution Committee, passed.

In a letter dated July 7, 1944, Dr. Rosenthal, a
member of the Bratislava Jewish office wrote: "A railroad
car recently arrived containing 15 tons of macceroni from
Hungary for the J.U.S. ("Jüdische Unterstutzungsstelle")

* For a complete account of the ICRC's efforts in Bratislava see their full report of December 1944 forwarded to the WRB in Washington on Feb. 1st. 1945.
A copy of this report is included in the JEWS IN
SLOVAKIA file under date of Feb. 1, 1945.

in Cracow. Our Red Cross (the Slovakian) received it
and forwarded it to Cracow on July 1st." These foodstuffs
had been purchased through the Joint Relief Commission of
the International Red Cross with JDC funds. A few weeks
later, to be specific, on July 18, Dr. Rosenthal wrote once
more: "Last week we received from the Red Cross (the IRC
in Geneva) a shipment of apple marmalade which we repacked
and sent on to the J.U.S. in Cracow. We try to get off
such shipments to them once a month which go through our Red
Cross and are officially cleared with the German Red Cross
so that they will be exempted from customs' duties. We
regularly receive individual acknowledgments for each lot
from our friends there so there is no doubt that the J.U.S.
actually gets the goods." A few days ago we were notified
that 20 cases of Lactocao (a Swiss milk product) were en route
from Geneva. Such products, particularly condensed milk,
are urgently needed since we can always use part of them here
for persons in hiding. Please ask our dear Uncle (Mr. Saly
Mayer) to do all he can to get us milk."

The above quoted lines bear strong testimony to the
valuable assistance for Jewish deportees in German-controlled areas rendered by the special food relief program
inaugurated through the ICRC, due to the Board's action,
early in 1944. Aware of the great need existing and generously
supported by the Joint Distribution Committee the WRB was
instrumental in obtaining a special U.S. Treasury license
whereby the Joint's contribution of $100,000 could be
transferred to Geneva. This fund, consisting of 429,000
Swiss francs, served to set in motion an extremely helpful
food relief program for persecuted persons in enemy territory,
and, after consultation with Mr. Mayer was employed, mainly
by the IRC's Joint Relief Commission (the agency specializing in the purchase and shipment of food for civilian relief)
in the following manner: 100,000 francs were "cleared"
into Rumania, where they realized some 33 million Lei, which

were used, in cooperation with the members of the local
Jewish agencies, by the able Intercross representatives
in Bucharest, Kolb and De Steiger, to purchase clothing
for Jewish deportees returning from Transnistria (8
million Lei), to buy foodstuffs (originally intended for
the projected voyage of the SS TARI but later distributed
in Bucharest as relief - 15 million Lei), and finally for
general financial assistance to the thousands of indigenous and foreign Jewish refugees in Bucharest who were
in dire need (10 million Lei). 229,000 Swiss francs were
used by the Joint Relief Commission to finance food shipments, partly of Swiss origin, partly bought in Hungary,
to the following places: Theresienstadt (July 1944), the
"Jüdische Unterstutzungsstelle" in Cracow (June, July and
August 1944), to the ill-famed concentration camp of
Birkenau in Upper Silesia (September 1944), and finally to
the equally bad camp of Bergen-Belsen in Germany (November
1944). The remaining 100,000 francs were taken over by
the pharmaceutical division of the Joint Relief Commission
to buy medicines, concentrated tonic foods (such as Ovo-
maltine), and pharmaceutical products. During 1944 shipments of these things went: to the J.U.S. in Cracow in
July, Theresienstadt in July and November, Bergen-Belsen in
October and December, Birkenau in October, and to the Jewish
Community in Zagreb for use in the internment camps in
Croatia of Jasenovac, Stara Gradiska and Gredjani Salas,
in November. An original plan to send medical supplies to
the concentration camp for Jews at Westerbork in Holland
had to be abandoned for lack of sufficient assurance that
the goods would get through or that they would be properly
distributed.

59

FOOD RELIEF FOR CIVIL DETAINEES IN GERMANY

Out of the close contact which this relief experience had initiated between the Board's office in Switzerland and the "Division of Special Assistance" of the International Committee of the Red Cross whose particularly difficult task it was to aid the many categories of prisoners who did not enjoy the protection of the Geneva Convention, grew the War Refugee Board's major food relief program for persecuted groups in Nazi hands.

In August of 1943 and again in December of the same year the International Committee, aware of the great need existing among the tens of thousands of men and women whom the Germans called "Schutzhäftlinge" ("security prisoners") imprisoned in concentration camps, addressed urgent appeals for help to the governments and national Red Cross societies of several of the United Nations, including Great Britain and the United States. The principal (and formalistic) obstacle in the way of a normal flow of relief to these detainees lay in the terms of the Geneva Prisoner-of-War Convention. Under its regulations, which had been accepted by the Anglo-American agencies of economic warfare, no food shipped through the blockade into enemy territory could be distributed to prisoners other than those "assimilated" either directly or by analogy (as was the case of the interned civilians of belligerent nations) to the Geneva Convention. This meant periodic visits by representatives of either the International Red Cross or the Protecting Power and a regular exchange of information relative to the numbers of internees or prisoners in the camps, prevailing conditions there, etc. The German authorities, for obvious reasons, were never willing to consider the Convention as applying to either racial deportees or to "political" prisoners (whose only crime was the refusal to willingly become a part of the "New Order"). The size and quality of

this category of detainees which numbered well over a
half a million men and women in the concentration camps
proper)* the conditions of dire need under which they were
forced to live, and finally the fact that by virtue of
resourceful humanitarian effort the International Committee
had succeeded in obtaining a measure of access to them for
relief parcels, made it imperative that extra-ordinary
relief action in their behalf be undertaken.

In the fall of 1943 with the few foodstuffs procurable
in Europe suitable for parcels the ICRC had begun a limited
service whereby next-of-kin could purchase packages for
their relatives in concentration camps. These parcels were
sent to individual addressees (insofar as such addresses
were known) through the parcel post system, each parcel
containing a receipt card. The percentage of such cards
which found their way back to Geneva was unexpectedly high
and receipt of the parcels was also confirmed by many grateful   61
messages from relatives of such detainees who wrote from
Denmark, Holland, Poland, Norway and other occupied countries.
Meanwhile the Committee's delegates in Germany and German
controlled areas diligently exploited every opportunity to
visit concentration camps, to work out some modus operandi
with local commanders for the distribution of such parcels,
establish contact with the men-of-confidence among the
national groups of detainees, and generally obtain all the
information possible concerning numbers of prisoners and
conditions and needs in these camps. Gradually a control

* The numbers of detainees in the major, regular concentration camps toward the end of 1944 were roughly the
following: Oranienburg 45,000, Ravensbrück 35,000, Buchenwald 30,000, Dachau 25,000, Mauthausen-Gusens 40,000,
plus a whole galaxy of lesser camps containing between
5 and 10,000 internees each: Flossenburg, Schiermeck,
Sangerhausen, Papenburg, Dora, Bergen-Belsen, Landsberg,
Gross Rosen, Stutthof, Auschwitz, Birkenau, Schliessfach,
Hannover-Stoeken, Hamburg Neuengamme, Kaufering, Muhldorf,
Allach, Floeha, Johanngeorgenstadt, Wiener-Neustadt,
Neubrandenburg-Mecklenburg, Zwodau-Falkenau and others.

system was built up and a measure of toleration of such
relief work elicited from the SS.

The food supplies available to the ICRC's Division
of Special Assistance (mainly purchases in Switzerland and
the Balkans) remained, nevertheless, tragically inadequate
to meet the growing need. The German occupation of Hungary
in March 1944 and the Soviet advance into Rumania of the
following months further limited the procurement of stocks.
The International Committee's renewed appeals for aid,
however, no longer fell on deaf ears. In May and June of
1944 the WRB's office in Switzerland urgently drew the
attention of its headquarters in Washington to the ICRC's
proposal that a sizeable stock of parcels from overseas be
built up in Switzerland for this type of relief. The Board
went to work and on June 28, 1944 was able to cable to
Switzerland:

62

> "Discussions between the MEW, FEA and
> the WRB have resulted in agreement to an experi-
> mental program of relief for distribution by
> the ICRC to persons in concentration camps in
> enemy Europe subject to certain distribution
> guarantees. This agreement calls for the ship-
> ment to the IRC of 100,000 standard food parcels
> per month for 3 months."

At this juncture a stroke of luck or perhaps bad
luck, whichever way you chose to look at it, brought to
Switzerland the salvaged cargo (which had consisted of
standard pow food parcels) of the SS CRISTINA, a steamer
carrying ICRC goods damaged by aerial attack and beached
at Sète in southern France. In agreement with the representative of the American Red Cross in Geneva a request
was immediately wired to the Board in Washington that part
of this food be acquired (the canned goods had all been
declared safe for human consumption during a 3 to 4 months
period), repackaged by the ICRC and despatched to the
concentration camps in Germany. Permission to distribute
these parcels was of course dependent upon the final
decision of principle of the blockade authorities in London

to allow foodstuffs shipped from overseas to go to
"unassimilated" persons in enemy territory. Pursuing
its efforts in this direction, the Board in Washington
cabled the American Embassy in London, after having
cleared the matter with the Foreign Economic Administration:

> "We feel that on account of the project's
> political and humanitarian aspects, the econo-
> mic warfare considerations which have hitherto
> precluded our making packages available to the
> ICRC for distribution (to unassimilated detainees)
> should at this juncture largely be waived. The
> amount of food which might fall into enemy hands
> could not effect the outcome of the war nor pro-
> long it. The desperate situation of the people
> detained in the concentration camps makes it
> increasingly necessary that some aid be given
> them, even though we may not receive tight
> guarantees that each package reaches the bene-
> ficary for whom it is intended. We suggest,
> therefore, the granting of blockade authorization
> for the shipment of 300,000 ... food parcels
> to ICRC for distribution on a trial basis ...
>   Please present this matter as soon as
> possible to the relief sub-committee and endeavor
> to secure a favorable reply."

63

The proposal for the immediate use of part of the CRISTINA
goods was also submitted and its value in being immediately
available for shipment from Switzerland stressed.

By August 11, 1944 the Board was happily able to
wire to Bern that the blockade authorities had agreed to
the Intercross' proposal for the despatch of parcels to
concentration camps. It was likewise agreed that a portion
of the reclaimed cargo of the CRISTINA could be used in
the same manner. The authorization to the ICRC covered
an initial lot of 300,000 3 kilo food parcels to be shipped
from the United States.

With enthusiastic speed the International Committee's
Division of Special Assistance made up some 55 tons of the
CRISTINA foodstuffs into 25,600 parcels of 2.15 kilos each.
These parcels were shipped during August and September 1944,

both to individual adressees (some 13,300 parcels) and
as collective shipments (12,300 parcels) which were distributed by the men and women of confidence of the national
groups, to the following concentration camps: Sachsenhausen-
Oranienburg, Ravensbrück (the women's camp), Buchenwald,
Dachau, Bergen-Belsen, Hamburg-Neuengamme, Natzweiler, and
Weimar-Schliessfach - names, now their horrors have been
revealed to an incredulous world, which have become synonymous
with the intentional degradation and mistreatment of human
beings at its vilest and most ruthless. The CRISTINA
parcels reached men and women, in descending order of the
size of the groups, of the following nationalities: French,
Belgian, Polish, Norwegian, Dutch, Italian, Greek, Yugoslav,
Czechoslovak and Spanish. With regard to the ICRC's individual receipt cards it is interesting to note that from 5800
parcels sent to the camp of Dachau cards returned bearing
the names (as well as the all-important matriculation and
block numbers) of close to 8000 individual detainees almost
all of whom had been hitherto unknown to the ICRC. Some
of the "individual" receipt cards had as many as 15 signatures
crowded into every available space on them by the famished
men who had divided up the contents of these precious parcels.
Such information was naturally extremely valuable to the
ICRC's DSA for the addressing of future shipments.

Meanwhile the WRB in the United States had arranged
for the shipment from America of an initial lot of 15,000
parcels out of the 300,000 scheduled. This batch went forward on the SS GRIPSHOLM and reached Gothenburg in Sweden
in mid-September. Shortly thereafter they were transshipped
to Lübeck in northern Germany en route to Buchenwald, Dachau,
Oranienburg, Neuengamme, Mauthausen and Bergen-Belsen.

During September and October the WRB in Switzerland
was fortunately able to assist in getting two other programs
for the relief of concentration camp detainees under way.
On September 21 the ICRC asked the Board to back up a request

from the French Red Cross (Algiers) to divert to their
political deportees in German camps some 40,000 parcels
out of a lot of 260,000 originally intended for French
colonial prisoners-of-war. This matter was immediately
taken up in Washington and London by the WRB with the
result that on October 2 both the FEA and MEW had signified
their agreement.

In the middle of October the office of the World
Jewish Congress in Geneva drew the attention of the Board's
representative to the plans of the WJC's Stockholm bureau
to ship some 40,000 food parcels purchased through the
Swedish cooperatives into German-controlled territory for
Jewish detainees in the camp of Bergen-Belsen and in the
ghetto of Theresienstadt. The Board undertook to back-up
the Congress' request for Anglo-American clearance on this
program.

In November the representative of the Board in
Switzerland had occasion to see a detailed report on the
frightful conditions prevailing in the women's concentration
camp at Ravensbrück. The author of this report particularly
stressed the almost complete lack of medical care or the
most rudimentary medical supplies. In the interest of doing
whatever possible to remedy in some small measure this
deplorable situation the WRB's office in Bern immediately
arranged for the procurement of 500 special pharmaceutical
packages which, with the assistance of the Joint Relief
Commission of the IRC, were sent into Ravensbrück early in
1945.

On November 25, 1944 the Board in Washington was
able to wire that plans for shipping a second lot of
approximately 224,000 special parcels were well advanced
and that they should go forward to Gothenburg on the
SS SAIVE within a few days. Then in December the welcome
news reached Switzerland that the unshipped balance of
the 300,000 WRB parcels, some 60,000 in number, would be
sent to Toulon on the SS CARITAS during the second half of

65

December for delivery to the ICRC in Geneva.

All such information was rapidly relayed to the ICRC which then communicated with its delegates at the reception points giving them the necessary advise concerning labelling, addressing and reforwarding. The Board's representative in Switzerland was naturally in constant contact with the International Committee in the setting-up of the various distribution plans.

By the close of 1944, therefore, substantial progress had been made by the WRB, in close cooperation with other interested agencies, particularly the International Committee of the Red Cross' Division of Special Assistance, in at least starting the flow of precious food parcels to the tens of thousands of famished and misused men and women behind the charged wire and in the bleak barracks of the Nazi concentration camps.

66 During the spring months of 1945 a rapid deterioration of the German railroad system set in under the heavy blows of the Allied air offensive so that transportation became, as had been foreseen, the most difficult obstacle to be surmounted in the satisfactory continuation and extension of the WRB's food relief program for concentration camp detainees and deportees. Due to the fact that Switzerland had been virtually cut off from the outside world for several war years such equipment as heavy duty trucks, fuel and particularly tires were almost unobtainable here. Exhaustive efforts, however, on the part of the ICRC's DSA and of one or two private relief agencies, as well as of the WRB to obtain trucking equipment in Switzerland for our parcel program met with some measure of success and half a dozen trucks were rented commercially for a limited number of relief hauls, one during April as far as Theresienstadt. But this could scarcely be considered adequate to meet the great need in Germany. In March, therefore, at the suggestion of and with the backing of the WRB in Washington, Board

representatives from London, Washington and Bern met in
Paris for conversations with the American military authorities regarding transport equipment. Although the great
push of the Allied armies into Germany made it impossible
for SHAEF's transport and supply section to release trucks
to the ICRC for WRB's programs it was possible to obtain
a special weekly allotment of gasoline and a number of heavy-
duty truck tires. These supplies enabled the International
Committee to assign certain trucks, particularly part of a
lot of 100 Renaults which the French government had made
available to the Committee for transporting food to French
prisoners-of-war and detainees in Germany, exclusively to
the concentration camp relief program for persons of all
nationalities. Through this aid from our army and the
generosity and comprehension of the French it was possible
to ship at an emergency pace about half of our Swiss stock
of 60,000 WRB parcels to Dachau, Theresienstadt, Mauthausen
and Landsberg before the final surrender of the German
armies.

      Early in October 1944 - to go back a little in time -
the International Red Cross had presented a formal note to
the German Foreign Office requesting that the Government
of the Reich give most serious consideration to extending
to all civil detainees treatment analogous to that accorded
prisoners-or-war and the interned nationals of belligerent
countries under the Geneva/Convention (i.e. "assimilating"
them). A similar approach was made directly to Himmler
in December of 1944 by Mr. Raoul Nordling, the Swedish
Consul General in Paris, whose courageous and energetic
action at a critical moment when the Nazis evacuated Paris
in the summer of 1944 had saved the lives of several
thousand political detainees in the city's prisons who otherwise would probably have been executed or deported. Although
no direct response was ever given to either of these approaches
it was evident that they had not been made in vain. They

67

undoubtedly paved the way for the conversations between
the SS and representatives of the International Red Cross
which began toward the end of January 1945 in Berlin. At
that time members of the highest SS circles responsible
for all civil detainees, political prisoners and deportees
in Germany displayed, in the course of several meetings
with ICRC men, a willingness hitherto unknown to mitigate
the severity of their treatment of detainees at least to
the extent of allowing more extensive relief shipments into
the camps. During February, March and April, in the interest
of seeing that the ICRC took full advantage of these ou-
vertures on the part of the SS, the Board's representative
in Switzerland was in almost daily contact with various
members of the Committee. The great interest of both the
United States Government and the War Refugee Board that no
stone be left unturned to bring all possible aid to the men
and women in the concentration camps was impressed upon the
Committee and its President on numerous occasions. Whatever
persuasion, pressure, counsel or aid seemed best suited to
the circumstances was applied or offered. Finally, on March
12, 13 and 14 the President of the ICRC, Professor Burckhardt,
went to discuss this question at some length with both
Himmler's personal representative, Kaltenbrunner, and with
various members of the German Foreign Office. The result
of these talks was certain opening concessions, the most
important of them being permission for the International
Committee to station delegates in all the major concentration
camps to supervize relief distributions and work until the
end. This constituted a most important concession in that
it would provide a channel through which that invaluable,
last-minute psychological pressure could be exerted on camp
commanders and other SS personnel in order to prevent final
acts of barbarity. To cite only one example of what this
meant. The presence at the camp of Mauthausen near Linz
of an ICRC man named Haeflinger, at the time of the Nazi
break-down, whose courageous intercession was applied at this

critical moment undoubtedly saved several thousand prisoners
from being buried alive in an underground aeroplane factory
where the SS commander, Ziereis, had received instructions
to trap them by blowing up the exits and ventilation shafts.

A second concession secured in the course of the
Burckhardt conversations was the right to evacuate from the
concentration camps women, children, elderly and ill people,
mainly of French nationality, although this was later extended
to include a few Belgians and Dutch. The basis of this was
a small exchange of German civilians whom the French had
interned in Alsace. Returning convoys of empty trucks which
had been delivering parcels to prisoners-of-war were employed
for this work and during the month of April 5 convoys
succeeded in getting back to Switzerland with a total of
about 1400 detainees, largely French women, from the terrible
camps of Ravensbrück and Mauthausen. This small number is
due mainly to the fact that trucks were a most inadequate
means of evacuating, over long distances and secondary roads,
men and women in terrible physical condition from prolonged
mistreatment and starvation.

While WRB packages were moving out of Switzerland
the larger lot of some 224,000 parcels shipped to Gothenburg in Sweden in December were being gradually moved
to northern Germany. Outside of some 40,000 WRB parcels
distributed through the Swedish representation of the World
Jewish Congress to Jewish detainees in Bergen-Belsen and
Theresienstadt, the bulk of our Board packages went through
the ICRC's depot at Lübeck to concentration camps in that
area, principally the women's camp at Ravensbrück and the
smaller men's concentration camp of Hamburg-Neuengamme
which, in the last weeks of the war, became an assembly
center for detainees and deportees evacuated there from
all over the Reich. The balance of these parcels undis-
tributed at the time of the German surrender were later used,
as were those in Switzerland, for continued distributions

69

to detainees freed from concentration camps but still
in great need. From Switzerland, for instance, WRB
parcels were shipped during the latter part of May, June
and July, through ICRC's DSA to Salzburg, Bolzano, Linz,
Uffing (in Bavaria), Lustenau and Vienna for distribution
in displaced persons' centers in these areas, especially
deportees on the move. Some 5500 parcels were used in
this manner at St. Margarethen on the Swiss-Austrian border
through which large numbers of liberated or escaped
detainees, deportees and forced laborers in very bad physical shape came into Switzerland during the second part
of April or later passed in transit for repatriation to
western European countries. This "post-hostilities" relief
work with our remaining WRB parcels filled a very urgent
and great need at a time when the Allied military authorities
were not yet able to cope with the tremendous task of
feeding the hundreds of thousands of displaced persons.

70

Similar to the diplomatic steps initiated by the
Board through the Swiss Government in an effort to offset
the persecution of the Jews in Hungary, numerous and
vigorous representations were made by the Section of
American Interests of the Legation at Bern through the
Division of Foreign Interests of the Swiss Federal
Political Department throughout most of 1944 and the early
months of 1945 in a sustained endeavor to safeguard the
lives of several thousands of Latin-American document
holders (mainly Jewish deportees from Poland and Holland)
still in Germany or German-controlled territory. These
unfortunate people were those who, beginning as early as
1942, had been provided by desperate relatives with the
passports and nationality certificates of certain central
and south American countries (such as Paraguay, Ecuador,
El Salvador, Honduras, Haiti, etc.) whose consular officers

in various parts of the world had been willing, partly for
humanitarian motives but unfortunately more often for
reasons of unscrupulous personal gain, to provide such
documents. Their original purpose had been to serve as
a travel document which might enable the bearer, who had
generally been declared stateless by the Nazis, and who
had received an entry visa for some overseas country, to
depart. It was simultaneously discovered that the Gestapo,
amazingly enough, often chose to consider the bearers of
such papers as bonafide citizens of belligerent countries
and to place them and their family members in regular
civilian internment camps. There are cases on record of
the German police excepting Polish Jewish families from
the most frightful pogroms in the midst of Poland and
shipping them half way across Europe to a civilian internment camp simply because they held the photocopy of
a Honduran passport irregular issued in their name. Since
it is quite clear that the Germans had no illusions about
the origin of such papers their action can only be explained by the fact that these people had some value as
exchange material against German nationals interned in
the Western Hemisphere. Such Latin-American documentation,
therefore, preserved many (some only temporarily, alas)
from deportation and extermination. In the interest of
taking every advantage of this fortunate, yet undependable
state of affairs (which had already been almost too far
exploited by various individuals and organizations), the American
War Refugee Board, through the Swiss Government which, Legation and the
along with Spain, was the protecting power for a number
of the countries whose documents these deportees held,
exercised whatever "preventative pressure" could be brought
to bear on the Germans. The technique consisted in
frequently and energetically calling the attention of the
German authorities to the fact that persons in this
category were eligible for exchange against German citizens.

71

Simultaneously negotiations for the actual exchange of these _ad hoc_ Latin Americans were actively pursued by the Legation through the Swiss Division of Foreign Interests. Due, however, to the extreme complexity and length of time involved in actually effecting such exchanges, a situation caused in large part by the unending obstacles raised by the Germans, and by the obvious necessity of first bringing out individuals either possessing United States citizenship or having a prior claim to exchangeability, it was only possible during several months of negotiation to extricate some 170 deportees holding such Latin-American papers. They passed through Switzerland at the time of the general American-German exchange at the end of January 1945. At the same time, nevertheless, the status of several hundreds of other Jewish refugees holding similar documents as regular civilian internees was preserved and they were able to remain in the comparative safety of the "Illags" or internment camps for belligerent nationals under the protection of the Geneva Convention.

As demonstrated by the case of the deportation of about 200 such Jewish civil internees from the Anglo-American internment camp of Vittel in the spring of 1944 it was never possible to know to what extent such preventative pressure through diplomatic channels could adequately protect deportees in this particular category. In the Vittel affair, despite months of energetic intercession through the Swiss Legation at Berlin to the German Foreign Office, both prior to and after the deportation of this group, no satisfaction whatever was obtained and no trace of the people removed found. Repeated inquiries addressed to the German Foreign Office elicited only the laconic answer of the SS to the effect that the deportation of these individuals had been ordered " in line with the general policy regarding the treatment of eastern Jews." This tragic episode is once more illustrative of the feebleness of the weapon of diplomatic representation. In such cases the

72

Swiss Legation at Berlin could only address itself to the German Foreign Office and the latter admittedly exercised only very slight control over the sinister operations of the "Reichssicherheitshauptamt" whose "Abteilung 4" under the notorious Müller directed the whole frightful program of the extermination of the Jews in Europe. In this we were beating against a steel door with bare fists.

Parallel to protective action in behalf of Latin-American document holders the War Refugee Board undertook special steps through the American Legation in Bern in an effort to assist another category of endangered persons in enemy-held territory. In the fall of 1944, at the Board's instigation, the American Legation in Switzerland was instructed by the Department of State to advise the governments of enemy countries - in this case Hungary and Germany - that United States immigration visas would be made available through American Consulates in neutral countries to persons in territory controlled by Germany or its allies for or to whom such American visas had been either authorized or issued on or after July 1, 1941 and who, since December 9, 1941 because of wartime conditions or enemy repressive measures, had been unable to make use of these visas and depart. This authorization, in order that its effect might be more widespread, was extended a short time later to include four other categories of persons: 1) the alien spouse, parent or minor unmarried child of a U.S. citizen, or 2) such relatives of an alien resident of the United States, 3) persons in whose behalf petitions for the issuance of U.S. immigration visas had been submitted to and approved by the Immigration and Naturalization Service, and 4) such persons for whom verification of last entry into the U.S.A. had been filed and approved.

Lists of a great many individuals, principally Jewish deportees, believed to be in Germany or German-controlled areas

73

interceded not only with the Rumanian but with the
Turkish, Bulgarian and Hungarian governments, as well
as with their diplomatic missions in Switzerland in a
persistent effort to promote the emigration of a sorely tried Jewish
minority to Palestine. The ICRC was especially active
in the numerous attempts to secure safe-conducts from
all the belligerents involved for boats sailing with refugees from Rumanian Black Sea ports to Istamboul or
from Turkish harbors to Palestine, in order that the
International Committee's insignia could be used by these
steamers.* Lengthy and difficult negotiations were carried
on by the ICRC, in which the American Legation in Bern
was very active, during several months early in 1944 with
regard to the steamers TARI and BELLACITTA; and even
though such representations were never successful (mainly
due to the refusal of the Germans to grant safe passage)
the delegates of the International Committee in Rumania
and in Ankara continued to assist in every possible way
with the problem of getting refugees safely off for
Palestine.

54

SLOVAKIA

During most of the period of wide-spread persecution
and deportation of the Jews in Hungary the situation of
those in the German puppet state of Slovakia was relatively
undisturbed. This was due in part to the tireless efforts
of an extremely able Jewish office in Bratislava, the
"Ustredna Zidov," under the direction of Mrs. Fleischmann

* For a detailed résumé of the ICRC's activities in this
  respect see the Committee's long report of April 24,
  1944 filed in the WRB-Bern documents: JEWS IN RUMANIA.

coming under this category were forwarded to the Swiss Government with the request that they in turn be presented to the German authorities with proper notification that United States visas awaited these persons in Switzerland. The Swiss authorities were also asked to signify to the Germans their willingness to admit such persons to Switzerland.

After the transmission of a number of these lists to the Swiss Legation at Berlin it became apparent, as born out by the experience of the Swiss representatives there, that the German authorities gave little or no consideration to requests made for the protection of non-exchangeable persons. The Swiss Legation accordingly recommended, in the interest of enhancing the protective value of this program, that such people be reclassified and declared exchangeable so that steps similar to those currently being undertaken in behalf of the several other categories of exchangeable civilians in Germany could also be applied to these prospective visa holders. On December 30, 1944 both the WRB and the Department of State concurred. The Swiss Government was accordingly asked to inform the German Foreign Office that all these persons were to be considered exchangeable against German civilians in the Western Hemisphere.

Although it is difficult to evaluate the positive results of this particular protective program certainly such repeated reminders through diplomatic channels that the outside world and particularly the United States were aware of the extent of Nazi oppressive measures against innocent men, women and children and prepared to take all possible steps to frustrate and counteract this persecution did act as a deterrent upon many German officials.

74

NORTHERN ITALY

The pattern of WRB action conducted from Switzerland for the assistance of persecuted persons in the area of northern Italy controlled by the Germans and the Neo-Fascists closely followed that in France. Two minor financial grants were made in September and November 1944 to organizations and individuals for courier service and intelligence work, while a third went in January 1945 in support of an effort at "political intimidation." A fourth minor contribution was made in May 1945, just prior to the German-Fascist surrender in northern Italy for relief action by the Valdensian (Protestant) Church in behalf of fugitives in hiding. Two major financial contributions went in June 1944 and January 1945 to support relief and rescue programs by Italian resistance organizations. And also as in the case of France, a small shipment of medicines and concentrated foodstuffs for persons in prisons was financed and shipped by the WRB in Bern in January 1945.

75

Although territory adjacent to Switzerland and one with which numerous contacts existed it was never possible to develop in northern Italy as effective programs of assistance as in France. This was due in large part to the active participation in measures of oppression of a much larger and better established indigenous group than had been the case in France, namely, the Fascist Party and later the Neo-Fascists under whom irregular police action went to even greater lengths of brutality. The battle waged for existence by a great many persecuted men and women was therefore not only against the Germans but against a large element in their own people.

The Jewish minority, both Italian and foreign, in occupied northern Italy was never large and at the time the War Refugee Board began its work could certainly not have numbered more than 15,000 souls at the most. The financial

requirements of "straight" relief for this broken Jewish
community were in general, as in France, fairly adequately
covered by such agencies as the Joint Distribution Committee.
The most profitable field of action for the Board lay,
hence, in financially supporting assistance of a less
orthodox character through underground groups for Italians
themselves and for such aid as these Italian organizations
could render to foreigners in danger for either racial or
political causes. Formal political pressure, such as had
been exerted in the case of Hungary was not possible for
lack of a diplomatic channel. The Swiss Government had
never recognized the Neo-Fascist "régime" and had no diplomatic relations with it other than certain de facto
commercial contacts. The Board in Switzerland did promote,
however, late in 1944, one "political" approach of an
unofficial nature although the Swiss were not involved.

76 This was done through a dissident commercial agent of the
Neo-Fascist "government", a certain Dr. Kiniger, who was
in Zürich and who happened to be personally related to
some of the members of Mussolini's clique in northern Italy.
This effort was initiated with the assistance of the Papal
Nuncio in Bern at the suggestion of the latter and of the
representative of the Intergovernmental Committee on Refugees
in Rome. The Nuncio, with whom the Board's representative
was frequently in contact on other matters, both facilitated
the exit and reentry of Dr. Kiniger as well as the latter's
contacts with the ecclesiastical authorities in Milan and
Como. Through Kiniger's connections it was planned to in-
timidate the Neo-Fascist Minister of the Interior, Buffarini,
and his chief of police, Montagna, by threatening them with
eventual prosecution as war criminals if they did not grant
certain concessions. Although our original hope of perhaps
even effecting the release of certain groups of racial and
political prisoners or at least obtaining better treatment
for them was never realized due to the fact that the SS
was then in control of practically all the prisons and camps

in northern Italy where such people were incarcerated,
Kiniger did secure permission and facilities from Buffarini
for the sending of medical and food relief on a limited
scale to the detainees in the Italian section of the ill-
famed prison of San Vittore in Milan.*

Major financial grants from WRB discretionary funds
were made in June 1944 and again in January 1945 through a
Communist representative in Switzerland of the Milan
Liberation Committee to support in particular the excellent
clandestine relief work carried on by the "Women's Defense
Groups." This organization which was active in all the
major cities and towns of northern Italy specialized in
aiding the families of men who had been imprisoned, deported
or executed by the enemy and in maintaining in hiding or
transferring to safer regions women who were in danger of
arrest for political or racial reasons. The "Women's Defense
Groups" also organized the sending of parcels to patriots
in prisons and camps to the extent of their means and procurable foodstuffs. Our contribution to their work was given
with the specific proviso that insofar as possible it should
permit them to increase their aid to foreign Jewish women
and children who were in constant danger of deportation and forced for the most part to live in hiding under deplorable
conditions.

A portion of this WRB financial aid also went to
various partisan groups united under the Milan Liberation
Committee for other special programs. Part of our funds,
for instance, helped to organize a certain number of prison
breaks, generally in the smaller provincial towns, which
during July, August and September 1944 resulted in the release of some 35 patriots either condemned to death or
deportation to German concentration camps. At the Board

77

* For a detailed report of this undertaking see pages
  7 and 8 of WRB - Bern financial report submitted
  under date of May 30, 1945.

representative's express request a sum of half a million
Lire was devoted to the smuggling of food and other neces-
sities to internees both racial and political in the deportation camps of Fossoli di Carpi near Modena and of
San Martino di Rosignano outside of Monferrato. Several
attempts through underground channels were made to "crack"
the concentration camp of Gries near Bolzano which, after
the closing of Fossoli, became the principal assembly center
for the deportation of Jews and political prisoners to
Germany. Due to the severity of the SS control not only
over the camp but over this whole strategic border region
no success was obtained. It was unfortunately not until
after the liberation of northern Italy that some of our
WRB parcels could be sent there through the International
Red Cross which also hitherto had not been able to bring
aid to civil detainees in northern Italy.

78

The Italian resistance, lastly, used smaller sums from
our WRB contributions for the purchase of food and other
types of relief for the survivors of villages sacked in
reprisal by the SS and Neo-Fascist militia.

Throughout the period of WRB activity from Switzerland
in northern Italy it was very difficult to bring many
persons north to safety although general assurance had been
early obtained from the Swiss police that all racial fugitives would be admitted. The obstacles in the way of this
type of rescue work were the same as in France: a mountainous
frontier, poor communications due to Allied aerial attack,
and frequent partisan activity which led to increased
patrolling and punitive action on the part of the SS and the
Fascists. Despite these difficulties the "Women's Defense
Groups," during the late summer of 1944 and again in April
of 1945, did succeed in passing over some 10 families
consisting of 27 persons in all.

As with respect to other countries the WRB's representative in Bern naturally lent all possible support, of a

liaison, advisory and communications nature to other competent committees and individuals engaged in similar rescue
work in northern Italy.

In the course of the Board's work in Switzerland a
second uneasy and rather distasteful affair which happily
met with a certain measure of success involving negotiations
with high Nazi circles for the release of Jewish deportees
took place during the winter of 1944-45. As in the case
of the difficult and lengthy negotiations between Mr.
Mayer and Becher of the SS the role of the Board's representative throughout Mr. Sternbuch's (as representative
of the "Swiss Relief Committee for Jews Abroad") dealings
with Mr. Musy remained essentially that of an interested
adviser. Whatever aid deemed advisable was naturally extended to Mr. Sternbuch and safe and rapid communications
with the United States were made available to him. As
his negotiations progressed the Board was also instrumental
in the granting of a special U.S. Treasury license to his
organization in America so that funds could be transmitted
to "back up" these negotiations. As a measure of security,
however, the Board's representative in Bern was named
joint trustee of these funds, a policy which had also been
adopted with other similar remittances (those, for instance,
received by Mr. Mayer from the JDC during the Becher affair),
to avoid any use of them contrary to the interests of
the Allied blockade.

The "Musy Affair" as it came to be known in the
Swiss press, reduced to its simplest terms, involved
several meetings in Germany between Himmler and other high
SS officers and a former Swiss Federal Counselor named
Jean-Marie Musy well-known in Switzerland for his pro-Nazi
sentiments and who professed to be an old personal friend

79

of the SS leader. These discussions concerned ways and
means of effecting the liberation of Jewish deportees in
German hands. Mr. Musy's motives in performing this service,
which were open to question, seemed to consist of a mixture
of the desire for personal gain, the hope of playing a
striking "humanitarian" role and the belief that he might
hereby obtain more favorable peace terms for the Nazis.
The results obtained, however, were a matter of more immediate concern than his motives; and Musy's actions were
successful to the extent of extricating one group of 1200
Jewish deportees from Theresienstadt who reached Switzerland
on February 7, 1945.

Other similar schemes, of a lesser nature, were
frequently presented to the Board's representative at Bern
by individuals and organizations, so that one of the
distinct tasks which developed in Switzerland was the careful investigation and evaluation of all of them in order
that the WRB in Washington might be properly informed if
and when approached by groups in the United States who had
been apprised of such schemes by their correspondents
abroad. In general these proposals were of a more or less
suspicious sort which turned on ransom or near-ransom.
They were usually characterized by dubious commercial
slants and by an almost universal lack of concrete evidence
that they would produce any results other than lining the
pockets of the unscrupulous individuals who promoted them
largely in an effort to exploit desperate and distraught
persons who were willing to go to any lengths to save
relatives and friends from Nazi hands. It was accordingly
more often than not the unpleasant task of the Board's
representative to turn them down as tactfully as possible.

GERMANY

Board sponsored activities in Germany proper outside

of diplomatic representations through the Swiss Government, our parcel program for the concentration camps and other organized relief shipments through the International Red Cross were necessarily limited by the extreme difficulty and danger of developing successful relief or rescue operations on any appreciable scale in this country. Regular relief remittances were occasionally despatched to Germany, generally through neutral diplomatic couriers, by such agencies of the JDC for the support of the few groups of Jews still alive there and in hiding. One such contribution from WRB funds was made in December 1944 to the Hechaluz for the maintenance of their group in Berlin and environs and especially to finance the flight of some young Jews to Switzerland six of whom arrived on March 18 their admission having been previously arranged with the Swiss police.

Although the extent and ruthlessness of internal surveillance in Germany restricted underground "resistance" activity in the main to local operations it was possible for the Board, through the "Freies Deutschland" movement in Switzerland, a group composed of German exiles of various political complexions who maintained fairly close contacts with Germany, to develop a modest but satisfactory relief program. Although the primary aim of the "Freies Deutschland" was anti-Nazi propaganda work, they were glad to be able to assist political opponents and victims of the National Socialists whose lives were in danger. Small Board financial contributions were therefore made periodically to this organization in Switzerland from June 1944 through April 1945 to support and develop the following types of work: 1) the maintenance in hiding of endangered political and racial refugees, particularly those near the Swiss border awaiting a chance to come over, 2) the smuggling of medico-food parcels to "Freies Deutschland" centers near the Swiss border for such persons, 3) the "passing" of these fugitives across the frontier into

81

Switzerland (which took place generally across the Rhein
into the canton of Schaffhausen), work which included a
certain amount of preparatory "smoothing of the ways," and,
4) the operation of an intelligence service concerning the
concentration camps.

All of these services, with the exception, of course,
of the parcels, were financed not so much in currency on
the German side as in kind. From the beginning of 1945
Reichsmarks as such had less and less value in Germany because
there was nothing to buy. On the other hand such small and
unobtainable objects as pocket knives, cakes of toilet soap,
razor blades, cigarette lighters, and cheap Swiss watches
were highly prized and of greater value than bank notes.
We have one case on record of a young German political refugee who was hidden by a farmer not far from Lörrach, after
the July 20th. affair of 1944, for over two months for a
Swiss watch which scarcely cost 50 francs! A second-hand
suitcase full of such barter goods was, therefore, smuggled
across the border about once a month; and human lives were
saved with what could have been picked up for a hundred
dollars in any dime store in the United States.

The intelligence service with respect to the concentration camps (and many "Freies Deutschland members had been
and were still in them) was more difficult to organize
and long in producing any tangible results. When they did
finally filter through they were of utmost value, particularly
in helping plan the subsequent shipments of WRB parcels
through the ICRC. It was exceedingly valuable in this connection, for instance, to have inside information on points
such as the following: the "ideological" and personal attitude
of the SS commander and the principal SS officers toward the
receipt of food parcels by detainees, how much of a "cut" did
they and other administrative personnel take, which guards
or block leaders could be bribed and which could be counted
on to side with the internees, which of them were open to
intimidation of later prosecution as war criminals, the degree

82

to which the "men-of-confidence" of the various national
groups in the camp had worked out a <u>modus vivendi</u> with the
SS on the subject of relief deliveries to their men, or
whether a "Schutzhaftling" was forced to sign receipt cards
for parcels he never received. Although it was long in
reaching Switzerland considerable information did come
through, particularly after January 1945 and concerning
such camps as Landsberg and Dachau not far from the Swiss
border, which was of great assistance in planning our parcel
shipments.

Characteristic of the secondary fields of activity,
not directly involving rescue and relief operations, in
which the Board in Switzerland could be of help, was the
work, for example of the "Dutch Jewish Coordination Committee"
in Geneva. During the course of many months this small
organization had slowly built up a very complete card file
covering practically all Jewish deportees from Holland,
whether of Dutch or other nationalities. This had been
accomplished by dint of painstaking investigation conducted
by mailing out thousands of registered postcards with
prepaid answers attached. These cards were directed
mainly toward Poland and Upper Silesia; and out of about
twenty sent off an average of one answer was received. Often
this answer consisted only of the stamp of the local
Jewish organization which, however, meant that the individual
in question was alive. Again a hastily scrawled postcard
would come back to Switzerland after many months but bearing
precious information concerning half a dozen relatives or
friends in addition to news of the addressor. All those
mentioned were done so by nick name or in veiled terms.
The Dutch Committee and one or two other organizations
doing this work developed specialists in this type of cryptic
correspondence who could decipher an amazing amount of precious
news from one seemingly innocuous postcard. Once then a
person's whereabouts was established with reasonable certainty

83

the address was passed on to one of the committees in
Lisbon which arranged the sending of those little packages
of one or two boxes of Portugese sardines which have become
so well known to everyone who has lived in occupied Europe
during the past several war years.

This excellent work by the Dutch Jewish Coordination
Committee was unfortunately inadequately financed so that
small, regular contributions from Board funds could happily
play an important part in keeping it going.

84

As was inevitable in the case of an agency with
official governmental connections such as the War Refugee
Board doing special relief work for persecuted persons at
a time when half or more of Europe fell into this category,
a large number and variety of requests, both relevant and
irrelevant, reasonable or highly unrealistic, from all
quarters of the compass, descended upon it. Although the
intention of not letting the "trees obscure the forest"
was firmly and repeatedly taken it was of little avail.
These approaches might be best illustrated by examining
a cross-section of the incoming mail, visits and telephone
calls during a typical week. The following matters, for
example, were called to the attention of the representative
of the Board during a week in April 1945: a list of
"reliable" anti-Nazis in the Cologne area whom the writer
felt should immediately be brought to the knowledge of the
competent American military authorities, several offers
of service from German, Austrian and Swiss citizens wishing
to receive jobs in the control system of Germany or Austria
(one of them was from a specialist in cattle breeding), a
letter from a sergeant in the American Army in the Rhineland
whose parents had been deported to Theresienstadt in 1942
and who wished to know how he could find out if they were
still alive, a telephone call from a lady who wished to

have a special shipment of food parcels sent to her relatives in the Illag at Biberach, a letter from a Swiss
insecticide manufacturer who was sure that the WRB would be
interested in purchasing several thousand liters of his
product for "its vast relief projects," a long memorandum
from a man purporting to be a specialist on the subject
regarding the difficult lot of refugees from Soviet territory who did not wish to return, a telephone call from a
woman who declared that under no circumstances should her
husband be compelled to return to Yugoslavia since he
would most certainly be executed by the partisans, a further
visit (despite protestation) from a man who had several
times in the past submitted a project for the resettlement
of Jewish refugees along the west coast of Africa - such
were the problems of a chaotic and suffering Europe placed
hopefully on the Board's doorstep.

In addition to despatching wires relative to the
more important relief and rescue operations in which the
Board was participating or particularly interested, its
representative at Bern also received and transmitted a
large number of "secondary" messages for a variety of
organizations and committees such as the following: the
United Lithuanian Relief Fund, the American Christian
Committee for Refugees, the Unitarian Service Committee,
the Queen Wilhelmina Fund, the Save the Children's International Union, the Self-help for Emigrés from Central
Europe, the National Catholic Welfare Council, the International Migration Service, the Friends of Luxembourg, Inc.,
the United Yugoslav Relief Fund, the Jewish Labor Committee,
the Union O.S.E., the Belgian War Relief Society, the
Delegazione Assistenza Emigranti of Rome, and the International Rescue and Relief Committee.

In conjunction with its work of extricating endangered
persons from Germany and German-controlled areas - specifically
the two groups of deportees from Bergen-Belsen and Theresienstadt, numbering in all about 2700 souls - the Board also

85

concerned itself with the "straight" (that is, "Straight"
in comparison to the primary task of the WRB - special
rescue and relief action within enemy territory) refugee
job of arranging for their evacuation from Switzerland.
This duty devolved upon the Board as a result of the
guarantees previously given the Swiss Government and
underwritten by the Department of State and the WRB - in
the interest of facilitating and accelerating the admission
of persecuted persons to Switzerland - to remove all such
refugees granted asylum on Swiss territory to havens of
refuge in Allied controlled areas. This job developed into
a most complex, difficult and time-consuming one involving a great
deal of liaison with various authorities and organizations
both in and outside Switzerland. A long series of discussions,
beginning as early as January 1945 and which lasted well
into the summer, and meetings took place with military and
railroad outfits, with SHAEF and AFHQ, with the Jewish
Agency for Palestine and with the Swiss Red Cross, as well
as UNRRA and the Intergovernmental Committee on refugees.
Boats and trains were ordered and then cancelled, welfare
personnel was engaged and then released - in short what should
have been a distinctly accessory task grew into a major
responsibility to the detriment of other more pressing and
important programs. The experience, however, was instructive
and indicative of the very complex psychological problems
inherent in the great task of resettling human beings who
have endured years of uprooting, mistreatment and life under
conditions which bore little or no resemblance to those which
we Americans accept as rock bottom in our social welfare
work.

Such was the fight on one of the War Refugee Board's
fronts, with its sorties and skirmishes, its trenches
stormed and its ground gained - and lost - in the uneven
struggle to succour and to save some of the victims of
the Nazi assault on human decency. Its successes were
slight in relation to the frightful casualties sustained;
yet it is sincerely felt that its accomplishments constitute a victory, small in comparison to that far greater
one carried by force of arms, but which nevertheless adds
a measure of particularly precious strength to our cause.

*****

RDMcC.
Bern, Switzerland
July 31, 1945.

87

PARAPHRASE OF TELEGRAM RECEIVED

FROM: AMLEGATION, Bern

TO: Secretary of State, Washington

DATED: July 24, 1944

NUMBER: 4729

This message if from McClelland for WRB and concerns Department's 2377, July 11.

Although Swiss entry visas were secured over two years ago and on June 2, 1944 were renewed Gideon Richter and his wife have not yet arrived in Switzerland. The report is that their boy is in Ankara now.

It may be that the German plane angle is a confusion resulting from the arrival in Zurich on the twenty-fifth of June from Stuttgart in a Swiss airplane of ten members of the families of Chorin and Weiss; Dr. Margaretha, wife and two children, Otto Henrich: Borbelye, wife and three children. False Swiss visas were possessed by these people who, as part of a ransom plan involving 54 members of these families, has been sent there by the Gestapo. At approximately the same date about 38 of these were deported to Lisbon in two German planes. It is reported from a reliable source that a portion of the price was a 25 year lease to the German Goering Werke of the Weiss industries especially metallurgical, and that in addition several million Swiss francs were paid although there is no confirmation of this last. In Vienna there remained as hostages Hans Muetner, Baron Alfons Weiss, George S. Kornfeld, wife and children.

From a reliable source it is stated that the Jewish Director of akcwseeauvs, IU, one Wilhelm Bielitz, organized the departure of these persons and is now trying to come here himself. Should he arrive in Switzerland I make an attempt to see him. In the meantime I suggest that Bielitz be contacted by the neutral attache which Department's 2276 mentioned.

The case of Chorin and Weiss is the most outstanding example of the current ransoming in Hungary of rich Jewish persons. It is reputed that the prices are over 100,000 Swiss francs per individual. Recently in Switzerland one or two intermediaries have turned up to negotiate such cases. The only individual which Department's 1946, June 6 and 2142, June 23 mentioned who after investigation of all those named turned out to have any useful channels through Kurt Grimm contacted one of these intermediaries on the thirteenth of July who departed for Vienna that evening to be in Budapest approximately the twenty-third of July. Around August 3 he should return to Switzerland with practical data.

It appears that according to indications which ICRC received on the eighteenth of July from the Hungarian Legation in Bern and earlier from a special ICRC delegate who around July 6 took President Huber's letter to Horthy, the Hungarian Cabinet met the thirteenth of July and agreed seemingly in spite of storm of protests and public indignation in Allied and neutral nations (not to mention Allied military successes and effect of bombardments Budapest) to consider permitting: the Jews remaining in Hungary to be given relief from ICRC; and supervision of emigration of children and adults to Palestine and of children up to ten years of age other places. According to the same source after the Minister of Sweden's interview with Horthy on the fifth of July all deportations have ceased from Hungary.

HARRISON

89

cc: Miss Chauncey (For the Sec'y), Abrahamson, Akzin, Borenstein, Cohn, DuBois, Friedman, Gaston, Hodel, Laughlin, Lesser, Mann, Mannon, Marks, McCormack, Pehle, Sargoy, Standish, Weinstein, Files

DCR:EMS
7-29-44

MAE-624
Distribution of true
reading only by special
arrangement. ~~■■■■■■ W)~~

Lisbon

Dated   August 1, 1944

Rec'd   3:56 p.m.

Secretary of State,

        Washington.

        2374, August 1, 1 p.m.

        Have given Schwartz orally conclusion Department's

2112, July 28, 5 p.m. This is WRB 131. He apparently

reluctantly accepts Department's decision.

                                NORWEB

Doc. 6

90

EH

EMB

Miss Chauncey (For the Sec'y), Abrahamson, Akzin, Borenstein,
Cohn, DuBois, Friedman, Gaston, Hodel, Laughlin, Lesser, Mann,
Mannon, Marks, McCormack, Pehle, Sargoy, Standish, Weinstein,
Files

KD-342
This telegram must be
paraphrased before being
communicated to anyone
other than a Government
agency. (~~RESTRICTED~~)

Secretary of State
Washington

4972, August 3, 9 a.m.

Referring to present situation of Jews in Hungary
Burckhardt of ICRC communicated to me message received
July 31 from Dr. Scnirmer (formerly in Berlin) and Bern
ICRC representative in Budapest substance of which follows.

One. Sufficient quantities of food and clothing are
available in Hungary. Funds will be needed, however, to
purchase foodstuffs for relief to recently dispossessed
Jews in Budapest and more particularly to those remaining
in provinces in camps.

Two. Jews in Budapest are now allowed to leave their
houses to make purchases between ten and seventeen hours
(formerly only between fourteen and seventeen). Those
possessing adequate means can purchase sufficient food
for their needs. The legitimatation cards of Jews in
Budapest expire on August 1. They will, however, be
granted new ones and according to recent decrees a certain
number of special work permits will be issued to Jews
"whose intellectual or physical labor is considered to be
of public utility".

Three. All internment and concentration camps and
consigned Jewis houses in Budapest will be accessible
to ICRC delegates. Schirmer and Born have visited twenty-
five such houses as well as hospitals and baths. In
latter satisfactory conditions prevailed. They also
visited camps of Kistarcsa and Sarvar on July 2.5. (According to additional information there are other Jewish camps
at Miskolc, Jasznereny and Pecs). ICRC Geneva will be
notified by telegram if and what relief supplies are
necessary for these camps. Transportation facilitias in
Hungary will be granted and goods consigned to Hungarian
Red Cross for distribution be ICRC. ICRC may choose
Jewish men of confidence in camps.

Four. Any relief undertaken by ICRC will receive
collaboration of Hungarian Red Cross and of official
"Judenrat" in Budapest. Final control of all distributions
will be in hands of ICRC. Auxiliary relief personnel can
be supplied by Jews themselves. Such personnel will be

exempted from

exempted from wearing yellow Jewish star. Adequate space
for officers and storerooms will be made available to
any ICRC Jewish relief program.

Five. About 8,700 Jewish families amounting to some
40,000 souls plus 1,000 orphaned children will be allowed
to emigrate from Hungary to Palestine via Rumania and
Turkey. An inatial transport of about 2,000 persons will
leave Budapest within next 8 to 10 days. ICRC will take
charge of departure transportation and care this convoy
en route. Born will accompany first convoy to Rumanian
port of Constanza. Boats are reported to be available.

HARRISON

RR

92

cc: Miss Chauncey (For the Sec'y), Abrahamson, Akzin, Borenstein,
Cohn, DuBois, Friedman, Gaston, Hodel, Laughlin, Lesser, Mann,
Mannon, Marks, McCormack, Pehle, Sargoy, Standish, Weinstein,
Files

PARAPHRASE OF TELEGRAM RECEIVED

FROM: American Legation, Bern
TO: Secretary of State, Washington
DATED: August 3, 1944
NUMBER: 4974

McClelland sends the following for War Refugee Board.

The following paragraphs are a continuation of Legation's August 3 telegram No. 4972 and complete the message from ICRC.

(6) It is expected that in connection with the foregoing the President of Hungarian "Judnerat", Mr. Samuel Stern, will leave shortly for Palestine.

(7) ICRC has received repeated assurances indirectly from the Rumanian Government (through channel mentioned in Legation's July 5 telegram No. 4257) that necessary transit facilities from Hungary will be granted for Jewish refugees, and that as regards the securing of suitable steamers the Rumanians will give further assistance in any way possible. Information has also been received by ICRC from the Swiss Legation in Sofia that the Government of Bulgaria is willing to grant such overland transit facilities for refugees as are necessary. END.

Carl Burckhardt desires to transmit personal appeal in line with paragraph five above and with the Department's July 28 cable No. 2605, to the American Ambassador in London expressing his appreciation and that of ICRC for any steps which could be taken with the British Government to expedite the admission into Palestine of these 8,700 families at least. It is strong feeling of Burckhardt that prompt removal of such refugees from territory of Rumania is essential in order to insure the Rumanian Government's continued cooperation in evacuation of Hungarian Jewish refugees.

Paragraph above refers to the Department's July 31 telegram No. 2630 last paragraph; and to Legation's July 29 telegram No. 4896.

Harrison

DCR:EBH 8/8/44

cc: Miss Chauncey (For Sec'y), Abrahamson, Akzin, Borenstein,
    Cohn, DuBois, Friedman, Gaston, Hodel, Laughlin, Lesser,
    Mann, Mannon, Marks, McCormack, Pehle, Sargoy, Standish,
    Weinstein, Files

This message was er)neously distributed as the complete message.
Section 2 follows.

PARAPHRASE OF TELEGRAM RECEIVED

FROM: American Legation, Bern

TO: Secretary of State, Washington

DATED: August 11, 1944

NUMBER: 5197

Doc. 9

94

We have already obtained Hungarian exit and Roumanian transit permission for the first convoy of 2000 people and it is reported that boats are available at Constanza. German exit permits from Hungary have not been granted and according to statements by the Gestapo chief made to Kasztner they will not be granted unless certain ransom terms are fulfilled.

When Joel Brandt's mission to Istanbul (please see Legation's cable of July 5, No. 4258) failed to produce concrete results and he did not return to Hungary but instead went on to Jerusalem, in the face of obvious German displeasure, desperate efforts were made by Jewish circles in Budapest to keep negotiations with the Gestapo going by raising goods and valuables from local sources to a value of 3 million Swiss francs and by stating that a credit of 2 million francs would be opened in Switzerland to cover purchased goods (tractors) there and in Slovakia (sheepskins). The affair of 40 tractors which Sternbuch brought to our attention (see Legation's message of July 26, No. 4802) was part of this deal which Link Freudiger of the orthodox group at Budapest negotiated and.

relayed

relayed to Sternbuch. On the basis of these offers, the Gestapo in Budapest refrained from sending to Auschwitz during the initial period of deportations the following groups totaling 17290 souls.

1. 1690 people of whom the 1200 prominent Orthodox Jews and Rabbis mentioned previously seem to have been a part. This group was sent via Bratislava to Strasshof in Austria and later to the camp of Bergen-Belsen in Germany where they are now.

2. Approximately 15,000 persons were sent to unknown destinations in Austria to be kept "on ice" as was stated by the Gestapo; and 600 persons are still confined in Budapest.

These various offers were made as a stop gap in the desperate hope that in the meantime Brandt's negotiations would be successful and thus render superfluous these make-shift deals. As Kasztner writes, we were forced to enter upon such negotiations to win time or do nothing. Apparently he was further encouraged by a message dated June 30 from BarLas of the Jewish Agency in Istanbul saying that funds would be available for the prevention of deportation and for emigration.

The desire was expressed by Gestapo represenatives in Budapest to meet Joseph Schwartz of JDC in Lisbon to discuss the terms of payment and release of 17290 Jews who were to be permitted to go to Spain according to the original agreement.

After

After the attempt on Hitler's life, the meeting place was changed to Irun on the Franco Spanish border on orders from Berlin and following the unwillingness of Schwartz to meet them at all, the Germans agreed to meet Saly Mayer instead as a neutral citizen at Austro-Swiss border on or about the 13th of August. As proof of their "good faith" and on the insistence of Kasztner, the Germans also unconditionally agreed to release the convoy of 500 people from Bergen-Belsen which would be permitted to come to Switzerland. Finally assurances were given by the Germans that until the question had been discussed with JDC representatives no deportations of the 17290 Jews would take place.

96

A Gestapo agent on July 21 visited Jewish groups in Bratislava who assured him 300 tractors were available in Switzerland. A very favorable impression was created by this news with the Gestapo chief in Budapest, since as is reported by Kasztner, tractors are what are most desired and used here. Before Joel Brandt's departure, the Gestapo in Budapest had declared that they were willing to trade 1000 Jews for every 10 tractors and even went so far as to give assurance that if the delivery of the tractors was begun seriously "they would destroy the 'plants' at Auschwitz".

It is my personal opinion, in light of this information, that Saly Mayer should be permitted to meet Gestapo agents (provided that his own Government, with which the matter has

been

been discussed, approves and grants the necessary border
permits for German agents) in an effort to draw out the
negotiations and gain as much time as possible without,
if possible, making any commitments. I recommended to Saly
and he concurred that preliminary message be sent to Budapest
postponing the scheduled meeting for a few days pending the
arrival of a letter to be dispatched on August 10 to Budapest
by courier, the letter to state in turn that no meeting can
take place before the arrival in Switzerland of the convoy of
500. In view of the rapidly changing military situation, any
time gained is in favor of the endangered Jews. On the other
hand, before Saly goes to such a meeting, we must have some
very definite expression of your opinion, in case it is impossible to stall, whether any commitments whatsoever on the basis
of either tractors, money or both can be entered upon. You should
also bear in mind the fact that the Gestapo chief in Budapest
has already declared that not one of the 40,000 Jews whose
emigration to Palestine is now being planned will be allowed
to depart from Hungary unless tractors are secured for them.
Concerning the first sentence of Department's cable of August 2,
No. 2656, I am not personally able to assume the responsibility
for final decision in a serious matter of this sort. However,
my own opinion is that apart from the manoeuver to gain time,
at this juncture it is impossible to embark upon a program of
buying Jews out of Nazi hands, especially in exchange for
goods which might enable the enemy to prolong the war. Further,

97

                                        there

there is no assurance that the Swiss Government would be
willing to allow the entry of Jewish refugees from Hungary into
Switzerland whose release ~~would be~~ had been secured by ransom payments.

HARRISON

98

DCR:VAG:EFR   8/15/44

FROM: American Legation, Bern

TO: Secretary of State, Washington

DATED: August 11, 1944

NUMBER: 5127

CONTROL COPY

McClelland sends the following for the War Refugee Board.

Reference is made herewith to Department's cable of August 2, no. 2656, and Legation's messages of August 3, nos. 4972 and 4974, and of August 5, no. 5043.

There has just reached Switzerland several reports dated the end of July from reliable Jewish sources in Budapest (Kasztner, Komoly and Perez) which shed additional light on the present situation of Jews in Hungary with regard especially to ransom and emigration aspects of the problem. In spite of the preliminary reassuring news of the agreement between the ICRC and the Hungarian Government to allow Jewish emigration to Palestine and elsewhere and relief to Jews remaining in Hungary it now seems that ranking Gestapo agents of so called "Sondereinsatz Kommand" specially sent to Budapest to direct the deportation of Jews have no intention of permitting them to emigrate freely, especially to Palestine, if they can prevent it. After the attack on Hitler and following the rapid worsening of the German military situation, the Gestapo in Budapest shifted their interest from the ideological aspect of Jewish extermination to the purely material benefits in goods, labor and money to be derived therefrom. The essence of their present attitude is contained in declaration of Gestapo Head to Kasztner to the effect that he

                                                        wished

Doc. 10

99

wished to pump out the necessary labor from Hungary Jewry, and
sell the balance of valueless human material against valuable
goods.

On the other hand, the Hungarian Government led by Horth
apparently has been frightened not only into stopping deportation (July 8) but also into trying to make up for the unsavory
role it has already played in the persecution and deportation
of Jews by favoring their emigration and relief to them under
the supervision of IGRC. Krauss of the Jewish Agency for Palestine accordingly has been permitted to set up an office in the
Swiss Legation where they are actively preparing the emigration
to Palestine of 8700 families previously mentioned.

100

                              HARRISON

MEMORANDUM

August 17, 1944

TO: Mr. Stettinius

FROM: Mr. Pehle

Cable No. 5197 of August 11 from Mr. McClelland, the War Refugee Board representative in Bern, discloses a serious development in the Jewish situation in Hungary. A copy of such cable is attached hereto.

The second section of the above cable, which was received by the War Refugee Board on August 16, indicates that while Hungarian exit visas and Rumanian transit visas have been obtained for the first convoy of 2,000 Jews from Hungary, the Gestapo has made it clear that these Jews will not be permitted to emigrate from Hungary unless certain ransom terms are fulfilled. The refusal of the Germans to permit emigration of these people is confirmed in cable 1479 of August 12 from Ankara, a copy of which is attached.

It now appears that despite the so-called Horthy offer and the apparent willingness of Hungarian authorities to permit the emigration of certain categories of Jews and despite the willingness of this Government and the British Government to find havens of refuge for Jews leaving Hungary who reach neutral or United Nations' territory, the Germans do not intend to permit Jews to leave Hungary unless they can extract either war materials or money as ransom for such Jews.

As I have previously indicated to you, I feel strongly that we cannot enter into any ransom transactions with the German authorities in order to obtain the release of the Jews.

You will note that McClelland suggests the possibility of a meeting between Saly Mayer, a Swiss subject and a leader of the Jewish Community in Switzerland, and the Germans in the hope merely that negotiations can be prolonged and time be gained during which the Jews will remain safe. The War Refugee Board would favor any such time-gaining device. However, in view of any political considerations which may be involved, I am of the opinion that the State Department must pass upon the nature of the reply to be made to McClelland's inquiry concerning such a meeting. A proposed cable to McClelland is attached.

Enclosures

Original sgd. by
Mr. Pehle
Copy to: Mr. Warren at State

(Signed) J.W. Pehle

JBFriedman:dg 8/17/44

Doc. 11

101

DEPARTMENT
OF
STATE

INCOMING
TELEGRAM

DIVISION OF
COMMUNICATIONS
AND RECORDS

RA-262
Distribution of true
reading only by special
arrangement. (SECRET W)

Ankara

Dated August 12, 1944

Rec'd 1 a.m. 13th

Secretary of State

Washington

102

1479, August 12, 5 p.m.

For your information (FOR PEHLE FROM HIRSCHMANN
ANKARA'S NO. 132) the Governments of Rumania Bulgaria
and Turkey have agreed in principle to grant transit
visas to Jewish refugees from Hungary who have obtained Palestine entry certificates. The two thousand
Hungarian Jews constituting the first group which had
been ready to leave Hungary had been expected to
arrive in Rumania some days ago. It is not understood in Istanbul why this emigration does not proceed since the Hungarian authorities in their announce-
ment stated that exit facilities would be granted to
Jews in Hungary for whom Palestine visas had been
authorized and Turkish transit visas approved in
principle.

Information received in Istanbul from reliable
private sources indicates that although the Hungarian

Government

Government has agreed to provide the necessary exit
facilitie's final authorization must be granted by the
German military and political organizations in Budapest
for the depature of each individual transport, and we
are informed that such authorization has not until now
been granted.

It is urgent that we know at the earliest possible
moment what actually is causing the delay in the departure
of this first group of 2000 Hungarian Jews in order that
we may take such steps as may be possible from Instanbul
to facilitate their emigration. We are exploring the
situation from here but suggest that concurrently you
request the Swiss Government and the International
Red Cross to investigate the situation in Budapest.
Please keep us advised of the results of your inquiry.

KELLEY

HTM

103

FROM: Secretary of State, Washington

TO: American Legation, Bern

DATE: August 21, 1944

NUMBER: 2867

CONTROL COPY

Doc. 12

104

From WRB for attention of McClelland.

Reference is made herewith to the Legation's August 11 cable No. 5197 relative to the Hungarian situation.

We have given full and careful consideration to the matters mentioned in cable under reference and for your information and guidance the following views of the Board are given below:

One. It is still the intention of this Government to pursue all means practicable to relieve the desperate plight of Jews in Hungary, however, ransom transactions of the nature indicated by German authorities cannot be entered into or authorized.

Two. If it is felt that a meeting between Saly Mayer and the German authorities would have possible effect of gaining time the Board does not object to such a meeting. In event meeting is held Saly Mayer should participate as a Swiss citizen and leader of Swiss Jewish Community, and not as a representative of any American organization.

The foregoing message has been repeated to Stockholm as No. 1671, London as No. 6661, and Ankara as No. 726 with this opening sentence: Following message is WRB'S reply to Bern

cable

-2-

cable quoted in substance in Department's August 21 cable
No. 2867 and is forwarded for your information.

HULL

105

WRB:MMV:KG

1 PARAPHRASE OF TELEGRAM SENT

FROM: Secretary of State, Washington

TO: American Embassy, London

DATE: August 21, 1944

NUMBER: 6661   1944 AUG 31 AM 11 00

CONTROL COPY

The following message is WRB's reply to Bern cable quoted in substance in Department's August 21 cable No. 2867 and is forwarded for your information.

QUOTE----------

Doc. 13

106

UNQUOTE

Substance of quoted message was sent to you as the Department's August 21 cable No. 2867 to Bern.

HULL

WRB:MMV:KG
Paraphrase: DCR:EBH:MEM   8/30/44

PARAPHRASE OF TELEGRAM RECEIVED

FROM: American Legation, Bern

TO: Secretary of State, Washington

DATED: August 26, 1944

NUMBER: 5588

CONTROL COPY

(SECTION ONE)

MCCLELLAND SENDS THE FOLLOWING FOR WRB'S ATTENTION.

We refer herewith to Department's cable dated August 21, 1944, No. 2867.

In St. Gallen on the twenty-third of August I had a long talk with Saly Mayer (referred to as SM hereinafter), and I informed by him that the projected meeting mentioned in the Legation's cable of August 11, 1944, No. 5197, finally took place at the Swiss-German border town of El Margarethen on Sunday, August 20, between SM, Isreal Kasztner and three German agents. The German agents arrived on the morning of the nineteenth of August, but it was twenty-four hours later before SM could see them. Border passes were not granted to either side by Swiss authorities.

The head of the German delegation (a member of German "Wirtschaftsamt") characterized the discussions during this meeting as "preliminary."

Substance of discussions which took place as reported to me by SM is as follows:

Delivery of ten thousand trucks, which could probably only come from

DECLASSIFIED
State Dept. Letter, 1-11-72
By R. H. Parks Date SEP 27 1972

come from the United States, was the backbone of the proposition
which the Germans advanced. The Germans, in return for the trucks,
would release not only the Jews still in Hungary but all Jews
held by them, totaling about one million in number. The reply
made by SM was that placing the matter on such a basis most
certainly would mean categoric refusal by the United States, and
he further stated that he would not enter into a deal which
involved the delivery of war material which could be used against
the troops of Allied countries. Another formula would have to
be found if the Germans desired to avoid such a refusal. It was
stated by the Germans that the proposition of ten thousand trucks
had originated with Jewish circles in Budapest and had been made
by Kasztner and not by them. When the Germans were reproached
by SM for desiring to trade human beings for goods ("Menschen-
handel"), they heatedly repudiated this accusation and declared
that they were simply willing to take up a proposition which had
been made to them and which was of interest to certain circles
in the Gestapo.

Permission was given to SM to talk to Kasztner alone. The
following picture of the present situation of Jews in Hungary
was painted by Kasztner. In Budapest there are some 170,000
Jews left. One extreme faction of the Gestapo (hereinafter to
be called Group C) was impatient to continue extermination and
deportation of Jews and had desired to begin again in Budapest
on the nineteenth of August. The attitude taken by Group C

(which

108

(which is Hitler's attitude) is that they desire at all costs
to liquidate the Jews even though Germany loses the war. The
present Government of Hungary is either powerless to act or indifferent to the whole question. Admiral Horthy himself could
be no more than a passive ("unbeteilygt") onlooker to continued
deportation of the Jews. The Gestapo holds all real power in
this respect. No emigration whatsoever of Jews will be allowed
by Group C. "Orthodox" diplomatic intervention or protests are
more or less useless and have no influence on the Group's plans
and intentions.

It is felt by other Gestapo circles in Budapest and in
Germany in general (to be called Group A) that the whole program
of Jewish extermination is undesirable as a policy and should
not be followed.

109

Himmler's faction (Group B), whose attitude toward the
Jewish question is more or less indifferent, represents a middle
course. This Group does not oppose the release of Jews remaining
in German hands, especially if there can be obtained for these
Jews goods of value to the Reich. Group B was represented in the
delegation which met SM and they specifically mentioned that
prior to the meeting Himmler knew and approved of negotiations.
SM was informed by them that it would cost them nothing to
release the Jews and, on the other hand, by doing so there was
something to be gained.

It was

It was explained to SM by Kasztner that Group B had to advance substantial counter-propositions in order to be in a position to offset Group C arguments. It is because of this that they accepted the proposals by Kasztner and agreed to negotiate regarding them.

It is felt by SM that the fact that such a meeting took place at all is a hopeful sign in itself. Equally significant is the arrival in Switzerland of 320 Hungarian Jews for which these negotiators were directly responsible. Throughout the whole discussion which they held to objective basis, SM saw no evidence that these men were interested in financial gain for themselves. They seemed to have quite a matter of fact relationship with Kasztner.

110

HARRISON

DCR:DB:FB   8/29/44

Section Two

In connection with
~~with respect to~~ /material terms proposed, the point of
departure used by Saly Mayer in arguing the matter was that
insistence on 10,000 trucks would certainly condemn the whole
proposal to failure in advance; therefore, what other proposals
would be made by the delegation? It was stated by them that as
a compromise they might find acceptable Allied permission to
neutrals such as Switzerland to deliver goods (machine tools
for instance). Should Saly Mayer be able to secure in principle
authorization to proceed, they would give him a list of goods
of interest to them which would be available in Switzerland
and other neutral countries. Hope was expressed by Saly
Mayer that goods which were not of such an out and out
military nature could be proposed by them.

Saly Mayer, arguing that it would take time to make such
arrangements and that decision did not depend on him, requested
a ten day breathing spell (until the 31st of August) and he
succeeded in obtaining from the head of the delegation a
definite promise that he (head of the delegation) would do
all that was possible to prevent during this delay further
deportation of Jews from Hungary and their extermination, but
he warned Saly Mayer that the time when the matter could go
beyond his control might soon be reached.

It is strongly felt by Saly Mayer, and I agree, that
since three precious weeks have already been gained, no efforts
should be spared to find a formula whereby we can gain more
time.

time. An expression of your opinion as to whether point has
yet been reached where it is impossible to gain more time,
would be welcomed by us. Is it felt by you that further steps
can be taken without commiting ourselves irrevocably, but also
without negotiations being broken off? While awaiting your
advice, it was agreed by us that Saly Mayer, as a preliminary
sign of willingness to continue, could ask the Swiss for permission for the entry of a German agent by whom further negotiations are to be carried on. It is felt by Saly Mayer/he should
have some form of evidence that at least $2,000 are available,
if necessary, in USA in order to keep negotiations going.
Various dilatory tactics of a technical nature just short of
actual delivery of any goods might then be indulged in. A
request to submit a list of/desiderata could be made of the
Germans. In the meantime Balkan political and military developments are increasingly in favor of affording these people
salvation.

HARRISON

NYC222120-C

JIMENEZ   HIAS # 89317   2695 RCA   8/24/44   8/25/44

HBE/RS SZ5414 STGALLEN 121 24 1720 NLT

TO: LEAVITT JOINT DISTRIBUTION   FROM: SALY MAYER
COMMITTEE
100 EAST 42 STREET NEWYORK
B7000,2283; B7000,6989   NSL

NOTE

OURS EIGHTYTWO INSTRUCTIONS SCHWARTZ CABLE 96 CARRIED OUT TO THE VERY
LETTER AND ALL MATTERS OF PRINCIPLE ARE BEING DEALT WITH ACCORDINGLY
STOP TACTIC EMPLOYED IS GAINING TIME STOP NO COMMITTMENTS ENTERED UPON
ALL THE SAME SOMETHING CONCRETE HAS TO BE DONE TO SHOW THAT WE ARE SERIOUS
ABOUT COOPERATING STOP THEREFORE IMPERATIVE TO KNOW IF YOU AGREE TO CREDIT
OF TWO MILLION DOLLARS AS FIRST INSTALLEMENT AND WITH APPROVAL OF COMPETENT
AUTHORITY STRONGLY ADVISE YOU AGREEING TO ENOUGH BEING GRANTED THAT WILL
PERMIT US TO CONTINUE NEGOTIATIONS FOR FURTHER TIME GAINING STOP FOR FURTHER
(CONTINUE)

Doc. 15

113

HIAS #
MENEZ   89317   2695 RCA   8/24/44   8/25/44

PAGE 2

HBE/RS SZ5414 STGALLEN 121 24 1720 NLT

TO: LEAVITT JOINT DISTRIBUTION   FROM: SALY MAYER
COMMITTEE
100 EAST 42 STREET NEWYORK

B7000,2283; B7000,6989   NSL

NOTE

GUIDANCE PLEASE CONSULT BOARD WHO FULLY INFORMED STOP LET US HOPE FOR THE

BEST

114   NOTE: SCHWARTZ JOSEPH J- 242 RUA AUREA, LISBON BA4600,7000,2283

DEPARTMENT
OF
STATE

INCOMING
TELEGRAM

DIVISION OF
COMMUNICATIONS
AND RECORDS

DMH-865
Distribution of true
reading only be special
arrangement. (W)

Lisbon

Dated August 28, 1944

Rec'd 10:27 a.m., 29th

CONTROL COPY
Secretary of State

Washington

DEPARTMENT OF STATE
DIVISION OF
AUG 30 1944
AND RECORDS

2648, August 28, 7 p.m.

THIS WRB 167. JDC 58 FOR LEAVITT FROM SCHWARTZ.

Gestapo representatives and Kasztner met Saly Mayer,
acting in his private capacity as Swiss citizen. This
was done with full knowledge WRB representative Bern, who
it is assumed has advised Washington.

The Gestapo man asked that Mayer put up fifty million
dollars to be used for purchase of material in neutral
countries. This is the Gestapo's price for the lives of
the remaining Jews in Hungary. They also asked that
neutrals such as Sweden and Switzerland be permitted to
sell and export these goods.

Mayer made no commitments and conference was adjourned
til August 31. Mayer's idea was to gain valuable time. He
thinks he should make an offer when meeting reconvenes.
Otherwise, he feels there will be a tragedy. He suggests
two million dollars, but with the understanding he can do
nothing about buying materials. Meanwhile he asked that

1,400

Doc. 16

115

-2- #2648, August 28, 7 p.m., from Lisbon

1,400 people from Bergen-Belsen be allowed come to Switzerland under same terms as 320 already there.

Telegram from Rabbi Ungar of Budapest states that unless agreement is made deportation 1,200 daily will immediately recommence.

Please instruct us if possible before date of next meeting given above.

NORWEB

JT

PARAPHRASE OF TELEGRAM RECEIVED

FROM: American Embassy, Lisbon

TO: Secretary of State, Washington

DATED: August 29, 1944

NUMBER: 2655

CONTROL COPY

It is stated by JDC here that the interview held with the Gestapo by Mayer was in an unknown town in Switzerland and was held on August 21. It is further stated by Joint that cable from Washington gave authority for this interview. ~~Because~~ Comment on WRB 167, Embassy's cable No. 2648. The instructions asked in the cable given above were whether or not (1) there is willingness on the part of Joint in New York to make the requested payments and (2) whether or not license would be granted under stated conditions by Treasury and the Department. Today there was received by the Embassy from a thoroughly reliable source information to the effect that a cable dated August 27, from the Hungarian Foreign Office was received yesterday by the Hungarian Charge d'Affaires here. The policy of the Hungarian Government based on new situation arising in Rumania was outlined in the cable. The cable stated that Hungary is only defending its frontiers at the present.

As regards the Jewish problem, the following is the substance of an exact translation from the text of the cable: Hereafter no Jews will be deported and the administration of

                                        Jewish

Doc. 17

117

Jewish affairs is being given to the Government of Hungary which will personally handle all such affairs. This is the regent's decision.

Considerable doubt that deportation of a large or even a small number of Jews could be carried out by the Germans any longer was expressed by the Hungarian representative here. While he could not be absolutely certain, he stated that he understood that during the last two weeks there has been in Hungary a growing opposition to the Nazis both in the general population and officially. Such opposition would mean active resistance to any German purification. It was also stated by the Charge d'Affaires that at the present time any large movement would be physically impossible. It is the opinion of the Charge that any transaction of the sort indicated in WRB 167 is only a Gestapo attempt at blackmail. Further information on this subject is expected by him soon and this will be transmitted to the Embassy and through us to the Department.

NORWEB

DCR:IDB:FB   8/31/44

2 War Ref. Bd-Pehle

FROM: Secretary of State, Washington

TO: American Legation, Bern

DATED: August 30, 1944

NUMBER: 2990

CONTROL COPY

TO MINISTER HARRISON AT BERN AND McCLELLAND FROM WAR REFUGEE BOARD

Reference your 5588 of August 26, 1944. Please express to Saly Mayer the Board's appreciation for the excellent manner in which he is handling a most difficult task.

The Board is in full accord with your view that it is of the utmost importance that every effort must be made to extend the period of negotiation and thereby gain time. The Board is confident that by adroit handling Saly Mayer can take further steps without entering into any irrevocable engagement, and can minimize the danger of negotiations being broken off. It should be made clear to Mayer that there is no possibility of obtaining any material of any military value. Mayer, however, is in a position to indicate that there are funds amounting to at least $2,000,000 in the United States available to him, and it is suggested that negotiations looking toward the payment of monetary consideration be extended as long as possible in order to gain time. However, no commitment to make any such payment can be entered into without approval here. We are not at all convinced that large monetary payments to the German Government would be successful, and under present circumstances, we could not approve any such commitment.

Saly Mayer

Doc. 18

119

Saly Mayer should inform the conferees that he can not (repeat not) hope to secure any authorization for Switzerland or any other neutral country to deliver additional goods to Germany without a more precise definition of the nature and quantity of the goods desired. Thus, he may properly ask them to submit, as you suggest, a list of their desiderata, so that he may be placed in a better position to negotiate for the necessary authorization. This procedure should afford at least one and, if the conferees are not prepared to submit such a list at once possibly two additional adjournments. When such a list is submitted, Saly Mayer can prolong the negotiations by placing the discussions on a technical basis. The foregoing are but suggestions and the Board relies on Saly Mayer guided by you to employ every possible dilatory tactic to prolong the negotiations.

HULL

120

9/2/44

CABLE TO MINISTER HARRISON AT BERN AND McCLELLAND FROM WAR REFUGEE BOARD

Reference your 5582 of August 26, 1944. Please express to Saly Mayer the Board's appreciation for the excellent manner in which he is handling a most difficult task.

The Board is in full accord with your view that it is of the utmost importance that every effort must be made to extend the period of negotiation and thereby gain time. The Board is confident that by adroit handling Saly Mayer can take further steps without entering into any irrevocable engagement, and can minimize the danger of negotiations being broken off. It should be made clear to Mayer that there is no possibility of obtaining any material of any military value. Mayer, however, is in a position to indicate that there are funds amounting to at least $2,000,000 in the United States available to him, and it is suggested that negotiations looking toward the payment of monetary consideration be extended as long as possible in order to gain time. However, no commitment to make any such payment can be entered into without approval here. Solely from the standpoint of saving lives, and aside from any other consideration, we are not at all convinced that large monetary payments to the German Government would be successful, and under present circumstances, we could not approve any such commitment.

Saly Mayer should inform the conferees that he can not (repeat not) hope to secure any authorization for Switzerland or any other neutral country to deliver additional goods to Germany without a more precise definition of the nature and quantity of the goods desired. Thus, he may properly ask them to submit, as you suggest, a list of their desiderata, so that he may be placed in a better position to negotiate for the necessary authorizations. This procedure should afford at least one and, if the conferees are not prepared to submit such a list at once, possibly two additional adjournments. When such a list is submitted, Saly Mayer can prolong the negotiations by opening discussions looking toward the removal from the list of articles for which he may claim to have no hope of securing authorizations. He may also request more details concerning other articles, and by placing the discussions on a technical basis, require the conferees to withdraw to consult with colleagues having more technical knowledge. The foregoing are but suggestions, and the Board relies on Saly Mayer guided by you to employ every possible dilatory tactic to prolong the negotiations.

121

*   *   *   *   *   *

THIS IS THE BERN CABLE NO. _____.

It will be appreciated if you will arrange for prompt clearance and dispatch in cipher of the attached cable to Minister Harrison at Bern and McClelland, from the War Refugee Board.

4:50 p.m.
August 30, 1944

LSLesser:tmh 8-30-44
LSL.

Miss Chauncey (for the Sec'y) Abrahamson, Cohn,
DuBois, Friedman, Hodel, Laughlin, Lesser, Mann,
Mannon, McCormack, Cable Control Files

PARAPHRASE OF TELEGRAM RECEIVED

FROM: American Embassy, Lisbon

TO: Secretary of State, Washington

DATED: August 30, 1944

NUMBER: 2673

Reference is made herewith to Department's cable of July 28, No. 2112, and our cable of August 1, No. 2374.

You are informed that this morning Mr. Joseph Schwartz of the Joint Distribution Committee departed by Clipper for the States. It appears that in spite of instructions not to have contact or communication with German agents, arrangements were made, according to Schwartz with the approval of the Department, for a meeting in Switzerland by Saly Mayer, JDC representative in that country, with gestapo agents, subject to the condition by the Department that Mayer appears a private Swiss citizen and not as a representative of an American agency. This meeting took place on August 21 (see our War Refugee Board cable No. 167, dated August 21) and another meeting is planned for about August 31. "Both Washington and New York are fully informed of what has taken place," according to Schwartz.

Since this Embassy learned only subsequently of the arrangements for the above meeting which presumably were made outside of Portugal and since whatever information may have been sent to the Department has gone through other channels, considering the dangers inherent in dealings of this character in general

and the

Doc. 19

122

and the obviously extortionist nature of the gestapo proposal made at the August 21 meeting in particular, it seems to me desirable to call these facts to the attention of the Department.

NORWEB

123

DCR:VAG:FB   9/1/44

PARAPHRASE OF TELEGRAM SENT

FROM: Secretary of State, Washington

TO: American Legation, Bern

DATED: August 30, 1944

NUMBER: 2989

CONTROL COPY

A cable regarding interview by Saly Mayer described in your cable of August 26, 1944, No. 5588, has been sent to Leavitt, JDC, New York, by Schwartz, JDC. *from Lisbon.* Given below is a paraphrase of cable commenting on Schwartz's message received from Lisbon Embassy dated August 29, 1944, No. 2655.

Begin paraphrase - - - - - - - - - -

124

- - - - - - - - - - End paraphrase.

The reply to questions raised in your cable No. 5588 will be made later today by War Refugee Board.

HULL

NOTE: The paraphrase of the cable from Lisbon of August 29, No. 2655, was sent to you on August 31.

WRB:GLW:KG

Paraphrase: DCR:IDB:FB   9/1/44

DEPARTMENT
OF
STATE

INCOMING
TELEGRAM

DIVISION OF
COMMUNICATIONS
AND RECORDS

KEM-533
Distribution of true For security reasons the
reading only by special text of this Dated September 6, 1944
arrangement. (   ) closely guarded.
Rec'd 7:37 p.m.

Lisbon

Secretary of State,

Washington.

CONTROL COPY

2758, September 6, 4 p.m.

This is WRB 180 JDC 62 FROM PILPEL FOR LEAVITT

Dealing as representative Swiss Refugee Fund,

Saly Mayer met September 4 with representatives Gestapo,

Held second session September 5. Saly states he has

received instructions from Washington to spend $2,000,000

with clear statement 2,500,000 is limit. He also says

he has instructions to do everything possible to

continue negotiations. He states he informed Gestapo

he could do nothing about goods, was simply negotiating

regarding money.

He claims safety Jews in Budapest assured through

firm attitude Horthy. Mayer now only concerned with

those outside capital.

NORWEB

JMS NPL

Doc. 21

125

PARAPHRASE OF TELEGRAM RECEIVED

FROM: American Embassy, Lisbon

TO: Secretary of State, Washington

DATE: September 6, 1944

NUMBER: 2760

CONTROL COPY

Doc. 22

126

Reference is made herewith to Embassy's cable 2758 WRB 180 and 2757 WRB 181 and previous cables on the same subject.

Kindly advise most urgently whether negotiations which the Joint Distribution Committee is carrying on have the approval of the Department, in view of the fact that the Embassy is being requested to forward these cables.

The entire situation is very disturbing as the Hungarian Charge d'Affaires here has just received a cable from his government dated September 3 reading in substance as follows: The Government of Hungary has no knowledge of and no part in any conversations which the Gestapo, either with or without representatives of the Hungarian Jewish Community, is carrying on with any Allied body, private or official. Some time ago deportations from Hungary were stopped completely and no incident affecting Jews in Hungary has occurred since the beginning of August when an incident which an inferior Gestapo agent caused was sharply protested by the Government of Hungary. It is stated by the Government of Hungary that it absolutely excludes any interference by any German authority in Hungarian Jewish affairs.

While it is realized that all facts are not known here it would

would appear that these negotiations do not now serve the
apparent purpose of saving the Jews of Hungary. The fact that
there is nowhere in the cables any indication that our Russian
and British allies are informed of the negotiations is also
puzzling to the Embassy but that may be pure negligence.

NORWEB

DEPARTMENT
OF
STATE

INCOMING
TELEGRAM

DIVISION OF
COMMUNICATIONS
AND RECORDS

BAS-77
Distribution of true
reading only by special
arrangement. (▮▮▮▮ W)

Lisbon

Dated September 11, 1944

Rec'd 10:26 p.m.

Secretary of State,

Washington.

2827, September 11, 5 p.m.

THIS WRB 187 FOR LEAVITT FROM PELPIL JDC 72.

Mayer reports that with the approval of the
Hungarian Jewish Community all Hungarian Jews between
14 and 70 are to be put in to 3 classes. Class I all
able to work who will be employed in industry. Class
2, all medically unsuited to heavy work who will be
interned in camps outside Budapest. These will also
be required to work where possible in agriculture and
light industry and will organize camps themselves under
supervision Intercross. Class 3, all completely unfitted
to work who will be sent to Jewish hospitals. Mayer
also asks immediate advice and instructions about money
asked for JDC 67. He claims this an eleventh hour
situation as next meeting delegation September 13.

NORWEB

WMB

Doc. 23

128

DEPARTMENT
OF
STATE

INCOMING
TELEGRAM

DIVISION OF
COMMUNICATIONS
AND RECORDS

BJR - 769
Distribution of true
reading only by special
arrangement. (SECRET W)

Lisbon

Dated September 9, 1944

Rec'd 1:15 p.m. 10th.

Secretary of State,

Washington.

CONTROL COPY

DEPARTMENT OF STATE
DIVISION OF
SEP 11 1944

2811, September 9, Noon
THIS IS WRB 186 JDC 71 FROM PILPEL FOR LEAVITT.

Hungarian Jewish community have offered to

repay after war whatever Joint now pays. Above

information comes from Salymayer.

NORWEB

EH:WMB

Doc. 24

129

THE OFFICE OF CENSORSHIP
WASHINGTON

BYRON PRICE
DIRECTOR

September 9, 1944

Honorable John W. Pehle,
Director, Foreign Funds Control,
Treasury Department,
Washington, D.C.

My dear Mr. Pehle:

We are holding in Cable Censorship three
messages relating to negotiations being had between
representatives of the Joint Distribution Committee and
the Gestapo regarding the release of refugees from enemy-
occupied territory.

Inclosed herewith marked "A", "B" and "C"
are copies of the messages referred to. Also inclosed are
copies of other messages marked "D", "E", "F", "G", "H",
"I" and "J", relating to this subject. These latter
messages have been passed by Censorship after reference
to War Refugee Board.

Upon their face these communications
involve direct or indirect communication with the enemy.
Unless such communications are properly licensed, we believe
they violate the Trading with the Enemy Act. They constitute a type of message that Censorship would not
ordinarily pass. But for the apparent interest of the
Department of State and War Refugee Board in these negotiations, we would not have consented to the passage of any
of these messages.

Since these communications involve a proposed financial transaction of considerable size, and in
view of the interest of the Department of State and the
War Refugee Board in effecting their delivery, we have felt
justified in feeling that the negotiations are approved by
both, as well as by Foreign Funds Control.

However, before consenting to the release
of the first three messages hereinabove referred to, I
wish to be assured of this interest so that I may know that
these communications and the negotiations involved are
receiving such sponsorship and approval. I will appreciate
your comments.

Doc. 25

130

DECLASSIFIED
E. O. 11652, Sec. 3(E) and 5(D) or (E)
FDA ltr, 12/19/75
By SLR   Date JAN 10 1976

I am also addressing a similar letter
on this subject to the Secretary of State.

Sincerely yours,

Byron Price,
Director.

131

CCC V WN NR 11

FROM STATE FOR NAVAL COMMUNICATIONS

FOR CHIEF CABLE CENSOR

DCR/C NUMBER 557

TELEGRAM NUMBER 2765 SEPT SIXTH SIX PM FROM AMEMBASSY LISBON

TO WRB LEAVITT

FROM PILPEL

2765 SEPTEMBER SIXTH SIX P

THIS WRB 183 JDC 68183 JDC 68 FROM PILPEL FOR LEAVITT

ANOTHER MEETING IN SWITZERLAND HELD AFTERNOON SEPTEMBER FIFTH AND

NEXT SCHEDULED FOR TWELFTH KAZTNER PRESENT MAYER INSISTED HE MUST

HAVE ADEQUATE ASSURANCES OF CONTINUE SAFETY AND ULTIMATE EMIGRATION

HUNGRAIAN JEWS INCLUDING ALL OF BERGEN BELSEN CHILDREN DESTINED FOR

TANGIER INTELLECTUALS SEPHARDICS RABBIS ET CETERA HE ALSO STATED

PAYMENTS MUST BE MADE ON NEW COD BASIS HOWEVER GESTAPOS FIRST

INTEREST IS IN MERCHANDISE ALTHOUGH SO FAR NO DETAILED LIST OF

GOODS HAS BEEN SUBMITTED GESTAPO INFORMED BY MAYER THAT HE HAD

HEARD SIMILAR NEGOTIATIONS GOING ON IN SWEDEN FOR RESCUE 4000

INDIVIDUALS BERGEN BELSEN ON PAYMENT TWO MILLION SWEDISH CROWNS

GESTAPO IN SWITZERLAND SAID THEY WERE SOLE NEGTIATORS AND THAT

THIS INFORMATION WAS FALSE

NORWEB

TOD 2032/8SEPT44WD

RED WN NR 11 CCC 2043 TS

DECLASSIFIED
E. O. 11652, Sec. 3(E) and 5(D) or (E)
FDA ltr, 12/19/75
By SLR   Date JAN 16 1976

132

CCC V WN NR 7

TO NAVY COMMUNICATIONS FOR RELAY BY TELETYPE

TO CHIEF CABLE CENSOR

DCR/C NO. 554 DATE SEPT. 8,1944

TELEGRAM NO. 2757 SEPTEMBER 6,4PM. FROM AMEMBASSY, LISBON.

TO: WRB; LEAVITT

FROM: PILPEL

2757, SEPTEMBER 6, 4PM.

THIS IS WRB 181 JDC267 FROM PILPEL FOR LEAVITT

$25,000,000 WAS DEMANDED FOR MERCHANDISE AT SEPTEMBER FOURTH
MEETING OF SALY MAYER. THIS REFERS OUR 62. IT WAS INDICATED BY
SWISS REFUGEE FUND THAT 25,000,000 MIGHT BE PAID IN INSTALLMENTS
OVER PERIOD OF MONTHS IF SAFETY OF ALL HUNGARIAN JEWS WOULD BE
GUARANTEED AND THEIR LEAVING COUNTRY PERMITTED. THIS IS UNSATISFAC-
TORY TO GESTAPO DELEGATES WHO INSIST ON IMMEDIATE PAYMENT IN FULL.
IN ORDER TO CONTINUE NEGOTIATIONS MAYER REQUIRES AUTHORIZATION TO
OFFER UP TO 25,000,000. HE HAS MADE IT CLEAR THAT JDC CAN DEAL ONLY
CONCERNING MONEY NOT MERCHANDISE. ALSO ANY PAYMENT BY JOINT MUST
HAVE APPROVAL OF UNITED STATES AND SWISS GOVERNMENTS. IT WAS FURTHER
MADE CLEAR THAT MAYER COULD DO NOTHING ABOUT MERCHANDISE ARRANGEMENTS
WITH NEUTRALS. DESPITE FACT THAT NEGOTIATIONS CONTINUED YESTERDAY
GREAT POSSIBILITY THEIR FAILURE UNLESS JOINT ADVISES IT IS PREPARED
TO PAY THE TOTAL SUM ASKED.

(SIGNED) NORWEB.

133

DECLASSIFIED

E. O. 11652, Sec. 3(E) and 5(D) or (E)
FDA ltr 12/19/75 JAN 16 1976
By SLR Date

TOD2003/8SEPT44WD

"C"

JIMENEZ HIAS 98319.   2695 RCA 8/24/44

HBE/RS SZ5414 STGALLEN 121 24 1720 NLT

TO: LEAVITT JOINT DISTRIBUTION   FROM: SALY MAYER

COMMITTEE   NSL

100 EAST 42 STREET NEWYORK

B7000,2283;B7000,6989

NOTE

OURS EICHTYTWO INSTRUCTIONS SCHWARTZ CABLE 96 CARRIED OUT TO THE VERY

LETTER AND ALL MATTERS OF PRINCIPLE ARE BEING DEALT WITH ACCORDINGLY

STOP TACTIC EMPLOYED IS GAINING TIME STOP NO COMMITTMENTS ENTERED UPON

ALL THE SAME SOMETHING CONCRETE HAS TO BE DONE TO SHOW THAT WE ARE

SERIOUS ABOUT COOPERATING STOP THEREFORE IMPERATIVE TO KNOW IF

YOU AGREE TO CREDIT OF TWO MILLION DOLLARS AS FIRST INSTALLEMENT AND

WITH APPROVAL OF COMPETENT AUTHORITY STRONGLY ADVISE YOU AGREEING TO

ENOUGH BEING GRANTED THAT WILL PERMIT US TO CONTINUE NEGOTIATIONS

FOR FURTHER TIME GAINING STOP FOR FURTHER GUIDANCE PLEASE CONSULT

BOARD WHO FULLY INFORMED STOP LET US HOPE FOR THE BEST.

NOTE: SCHWARTZ JOSEPH J 2 RUA AURE , LISBON BA4600,7000,2283

134

"D"

CCC V WN NR 8

TO NAVY COMMUNICATIONS FOR RELAY BY TELETYPE

TO CHIEF CABLE CENSOR

DCR/C NO 527 DATE AUGUST 30, QORR

TELEGRAM NO 2648, AUGUST 28, U PM FROM AMEMBASSY LISBON

TO WRB: LEAVITT

FROM SCHWARTZ

THE FOLLOWING MESSAGE RECEIVED FROM LISBON DATED AUGUST

DATED AUGUST 28 QORR RECEIVED 1027 AM 29TH

THIS WRB 167. JDC 58 FOR LEAVITT FROM SCHWARTZ

GESTAPO REPRESENTATIVES AND KASZNTER MET SALY MAYER, ACTING IN
HIS PRIVATE CAPACITY AS SWISS CITIZEN. THIS WAS DONE WITH FULL KNOW-
LEDGE WRB REPRESENTATIVE BERN, WHO IT IS ASSUMED HAS ADIVSED WASH.
THE GESTAPO MAN ASKED THAT MAYER PUT UP FIFTY MILLION DOLLARS TO BE
USED FOR PURCHASE OF MATERIAL IN NEUTRAL COUNTRIES. THIS IS THE
GESTAPO'S PRICE FOR THE LIVES OF THE REMAINING JEWS IN HUNGARY.
THEY ALSO ASKED THAT NEURTALS SUCH AS SWEDEN AND SWITZERLAND BE PER-
MITTED TO SELL AND EXPORT THESE GOODS MAYER MADE NO COMMITTMENTS AND
CONFERENCE WAS ADJOURNED TILL AUGUST 31. MAYER'S IDEA WAS TO GAIN
VALUABLE TIME. HE THINKS HE SHOULD MAKE AN OFFER WHEN MEETING REC-
ONVENES. OTHERWISE, HE FEELS THERE WILL BE A TRAGEDY. H. SUGGESTS TWO
MILLION DOLLARS, BUT WITH THE UNDERSTANDING HE CAN DO NOTHING ABOUT
BUYING MATERIALS. MEANWHILE HE ASKED THAT 1,400 PEOPLE FROM BERGEN
BELSEN BE ALLOWED COME TO SWITZERLAND UNDER SAME TERMS AS 320 ALREADY
THERE. TELEGRAM FROM RABBI UNGAR OF BUDAPEST STATES HAT UNLESS
ARGEEMENT IS MADE DEPORTATION 1,200 DAILY WILL IMMEDIATELY RECOMMENCE
PLEASE INSTRUCT US IF POSSIBLE BEFORE DATE OF NEXT MEETING GIVEN
ABOVE.

(SIGNED) NORWEB

135

CCG   7-31-44

1. TAG/RS TY482 BEYOGLU 223/222 29 1835

2. JOSE MIRELMAN 1750 CALLE HEREADIA BUENOSAIRES

3. RECEIVED TWOTHOUSAND THANKS STOP RUMANIAN JEWS ASKED AGENCY TO STATE
IT WILL GRANT CERTIFECATES ANY REFUGEES REACHING TURKEY OTHERWISE RUMAN-
IAN GOVERNMENT PREVENTS EXIT THOUGH SHIPS AVAILABLE STOP AGENCY REFUSED
DESIRING TO KEEP MONOPOLY OF RESCUE STOP THIS POLICY FORCES OTHER RUMANI-
AN JEWISH ORGANIZATIONS TO FIGHT AGENCY RESULTING IN UNNECESSARY DIFFI-
CULTIES EVEN FOR AGENCYS BOATS STOP I HAVE PROTESTED STOP AGENCY DISCRIM-
INATION AGAINST ORTHODOX AND POLISH REFUGEES FORCED REPRESENTATIVES AGU-
DAH AND AMERICAN INTERNATIONAL RESCUE AND RELIEF COMMITTED DECIDE TO
SEND SPECIAL SHIP STOP AGENCY REFUSED PROMISE OF CERTIFICATES STOP
HIRSCHMANN INTERVENED OVER HEAD OF AGENCY PROMISING VISAS STOP HIRSCH-
MAN REQUESTED ME HELP ARRANGE THIS SHIP STOP NO DISCRIMINATION AGAINST
REVISIONISTS BECAUSE THEY ARE CONSIDERABLE POWER RUMANIA STOP ON MAY
NINETEEN BUDAPEST JEW JOEL BRAND ARRIVED ISTANBUL WITH PROPOSAL FROM
GESTAPO STOP AGENCY SENT BRAND TO PALESTINE INTO BRITISH CUSTODY
INSTEAD OF SENDING HIM BACK WITH ANSWER STOP AGENCY PROBABLY ACTED ON
BRITISH REQUEST BUT ACTION RESULTED AOVIDABLE DEPORTATION FUOURHUNDRED
THOUSAND JEWS STOP I AM NOW SENDING SHIP TO RESCUE THOUSAND HUNGARIAN
JEWS STOP APPROACHED JOINT DIRECTIOR SCHWARTZ BUT HE UNINTERESTED STOP
BELIEVE JOINT PREFERE DEAL AGENCY BECAUSE UNITED JEWISH APPEAL CONTROLLED
BY JOINT WHILE EMERGENCY COMMITTEE INDEPENDENT STOP MY PROJECT NEEDS
HOUNDREDTHOUSAND STOP CABLE ALL THIS INFORMATION BERGSON AND HELP SECURE
NEEDED FUNDS URGENT ACKNOWLEDGE

4. ERI JABOTINSKY

5. MM PASSED FWDD FYI ATTN CONTACT FOR STATE

136

DECLASSIFIED
E. O. 11652, Sec. 3(E) and 5(D) or (E)
FDA ltrs 12/19/75
By SLR   Date JAN 16 1976

7. RCAC

0800 CNY 174325 WIK

137

SCHILLER   HIAS   4031 ITT   7/21/44   7/22/44
                  86264

DOR, MA

RB41 VIA MKT RB NEWYORK NY 56 21 532ᵖ ORD

TO: FROM:
SILVERMAN EASTERMAN BAROU   MAURICE PERLZWEIG
55 NEW CAVENDISH STREET   (WORLD JEWISH CONGRESS
LONDON   1834 BWAY, NYC)
NOTE: B7000; F7000   SWI/154 YN 4601; BA4600,7000

                          NOTES

        NUMBER 135 YOUR NUMBER 307 GOLDMANN HANDLE HUNGARIAN RESCUE SUGGESTION

HERE COMMUNICATED ALTERNATIVE PROPOSAL SHERTOK WHOM HE REQUESTS YOU CON-

TACT STOP RECEIVED ALSO YOUR CABLE ON VATICAN AND OTHER ACTION WHICH

APPRECIATE STOP SIMILAR ACTION TAKEN HERE KUBOWITZKI SENDING YOU FURTHER

INFORMATION THROUGH WAR REFUGEE BOARD

CENSOR
THE FIRST PART OF THIS MESSAGE IS IN REPLY TO A REQUEST FOR INFORMATION
ON THE RECENTLY PUBLISHED REPORT THAT THERE HAD BEEN RECEIVED A PROPOSAL
FROM HUNGARY SUGGESTING THE EXCHANGE OF JEWISH REFUGEES FOR SUPPLIES DR
GOLDMANN WHO HAS BEEN DISCUSSING THIS PROBLEM WITH THE STATE DEPT AND
WAR REFUGEE BOARD REQUESTS THAT OUR LONDON OFFICE CONTACT MR SHERTOK
WHO HAS BEEN DEALING WITH THE MATTER IN THAT CITY WE ALSO ACKNOWLEDGE
A CABLE GIVING US INFORMATION OF CX ACTION TAKEN BY THE VATICAN AND
OTHER AUTHORITIES TO INDUCE THE HUNGARIAN PEOPLE TO RESIST THE GERMAN
TERROR AGAINST THE JEWS DR KUBOWITZKI WHO IS IN CHARGE OF OUR RESCUE
DEPARTMENT IS ASKING THE WAR REFUGEE BOARD IN WASHINGTON TO TRANSMIT
A MESSAGE TO OUR LONDON OFFICE ON THE SIMILAR STEPS WHICH ARE BEING
TAKEN HERE

NOTE ON RECEIVER:
SILVERMAN, NATHAN - GROVE ST CEDARHURST, LI, NY OR NYC BA 4600, 5359

NOTES ON TEXT:
KUBOWITZKI, LEON - 330 W 42 ST NYC - BA 7500
SHERTOK, MOSHE - 41 E 42ND ST NYC & JERUSALEM - SWI / 154 YN 4601, 7468

138

"G"

CONFIDENTIAL   NYC 145765C

SCHWEITZER   HIAS
                    86539   1308 ITT   7/20   7/25/55

DOR A N

CAXL258 XY LONDON 32 20 NFT NLT

TO: NAHUM GOLDMANN

JEWISH AGENCY 342 MADISON

AVENUE NEWYORKCITYNY   FROM: MOSHE SHERTOK

SWI/154 BN7000,4601,3837 NSL   SWI/154 YN 4601 7468 NOTE 1
                    NOTE 2 4 NSL

KASTNER INFORMED DOBKIN ASHKENAZI PREPARED MEET HIM AND
SCHWARTZ LISBON STOP REACTION HERE NEGATIVE STOP SUGGEST YOU
ASCERTAIN REACTION YOUR END

NOTE 1 - LISTED IN NYC & JERUSALEM

NOTE 2 - SCHWARTZ JOSEPH J 242 rue CUEREA
             LISBON PORTUGAL BA 4600,7000,2283

NOTE 3 - JEWISH AGENCY FOR PALESTINE JERUSALEM Y7468

NOTE 4 - DOBKIN ELIAHU OR ELIAS OR A-C/O JEWISH AGENCY
             JERUSALEM B7000

139

CCC N WN NR 16

TO NAVY COMMUNICATIONS FOR RELAY BY TELETYPE TO CHIEF CABLE CENSOR

DCR/C NO 379

TELEGRAM NO 97 JULY 11 YPM FROM AMERICAN CONSUL GENERAL JERUSALEM

TO   NAHUM GOLDMAN WRB

FROM   BENGURION CHAIRMAN JEWISH AGENCY EXECUTIVE.

I HAVE BEEN ASKED BY BENGURION, CHAIRMAN OF THE JEWISH

AGENCY EXECUTIVE, TO TRANSMIT THROUGH THE WAR REFUGEE BOARD THE

FOLLOWING MESSAGE TO NAHUM GOLDMAN:

ON BEHALF OF THE JEWISH AGENCY EXECUTIVE, PLEASE TRANSMIT

TO PRESIDENT ROOSEVELT THE FOLLOWING:

A PROPOSAL EMANATING FROM APPARENTLY INFLUENTIAL ENEMY SOURCES

AT BUDAPEST HAS BEEN RECEIVED BY THIS AGENCY. THE READINESS OF

THE NAZIS TO RELEASE ONEMILLION HUNGARIAN RUMANIAN JEWS, ON

THE CONDITION KNOWN TO THE DEPARTMENT OF STATE AND PROPOSING

NEGOTIATIONS TO THAT END IS INDICATED IN THIS PROPOSAL.

JEWISH AGENCY IMMEDIATELY TRANSMITTED THIS PROPOSAL TO THE

GOVERNMENTS OF AMERICA AND BRITAIN. A WELL KNOWN BUDAPEST

ZIONIST WAS THE JEWISH EMISSARY WHOM THE NAZIS SENT WITH THIS

PROPOSAL. AT THE PRESENT TIME HE IS DETAINED IN CAIRO BY

BRITISH SECURITY AUTHORITIES. THE JEWISH AGENCY EARNESTLY APPEALS

TO YOU NOT TO ALLOW THIS UNIQUE AND POSSIBLY LAST CHANCE OF SAVING

THE REMAINS OF EUROPEAN JEWRY TO BE LOST ALTHOUGH IT IS FULLY

REALIZED THAT THE EXIGENCIES OF WAR ARE PRIMARY CONSIDERATION. EVEN

IF THERE MAY BE SOME DOUBTS CONCERNING THE PROPOSAL IN ITS PRESENT

FORM WE WOULD URGENTLY AND RESPECTFULLY SUBMIT THAT SUITABLE

ARRANGEMENTS BE MADE TO DISCUSS THE PROPOSAL WITH REPRESENTATIVES

140

OF THE ENEMY GROUP FROM WHICH IT EMANATED, AND THAT THE DOOR SHOULD NOT BE
CLOSED. THEREFORE WE PLEAD THAT YOU MAY SEE FIT TO GIVE YOUR
SUPPORT TO THE FOLLOWING PROPOSALS WHICH THE JEWISH AGENCY HAS
ALSO SUBMITTED TO THE GOVERNMENT OF BRITAIN: (1) THROUGH
APPROPRIATE CHANNELS TO INTIMATE TO OTHER SIDE IMMEDIATELY, READINESS
TO NOMINATE REPRESENTATIVE TO DISCUSS RESCUE AND TRANSFER THE
LARGEST NUMBER OF JEWS POSSIBLE, AND (2) TO INTIMATE TO THE
OTHER SIDE THAT THE PRELIMINARY CONDITION TO ANY DISCUSSION IS
THE DISCONTINUANCE OF DEPORTATIONS IMMEDIATELY

    PINKERTON.

TCT1906Y 15JULY

141

CCC V WN NR 9

SD WASHINGTON DC 23 605P

TO NAVY COMMUNICATIONS FOR RELAY BY TELETYPE

TO CHIEF CABLE CENSOR

DCR/C NI 328 DATE JUNE 22 1944

TELEGRAM NO 82 JUNE 19 6 PM FROM CONSUL GENERAL JERUSALEM

TO NAHUM GOLDMAN

FROM SHERTOK

CONFIDENTIAL

IT IS REQUESTED BY SHERTOK THAT NAHUM GOLDMANN RECEIVE

THE SUBSTANCE OF THE FOLLOWINGMESSAGE

THE BRITISH EMBASSY HAS POBABLY INFORMED YOU OF

THE OFFER BY THE NAZIS TO EVACUATE PRIMARILY FROM

HUNGARY THE REMANANTS OF EUROPEAN JEWRY JOEL BRANDT

TRUSTED HUNGARIAN ZIONIST BROUGHT THE MESSAGE AND WAS SENT TO

ISTANBUL MAY 19 ON WEHRMACHT PLANE WITH A VIEW

TO RETURN WITHIN TWO OR THREE WEEKS WITH THE REPLY

THE OFFER OSTENSIBLY WAS TO EXCHANGE JEWS FOR GOODS

OF SPECIFID KINDS AND AMOUNTS THE EVACUEES WERE TO

PROCEED TO SPAIN ON RECEIPT OF FAVORABLE REPLY CONCERNING

THE WHOLE SCHEME THE FIRST SUBSTANTIAL TRANSPORT

WAS TO BE SENT OUT WITHOUT CONSIDERATION THE CONDITIONS

OF THE EXCHANGE SOUNDED FANTASTIC BUT IT WAS DECIDED TO

EXPLORE IT WE IMMEDIATELY INFORMED THE HIGH COMMISSIONER

142

WHO REPORTED TO LONDON IN FULL WITH REQUEST THAT

WASHINGTON AND YOU BE ADVISED EVERY POSSIBLE AID WAS

GIVEN BY THE COMMISSIONER TO ASSIST ME TO PROCEED TO

TURKEY FOR THE PURPOSE OF INTERVIEWING BRANDT MY DEPARTURE WAS

DELAYEDNBECAUSE OF VISA DIFFICULTIES (ASTERISK) SD AUTHORITIES

JERUSALEM ISTANBUL THAT BRANDT

SHOULD RETURN TO TURKEY WITH A VIEW TO PROCEED TO HUNGARY

FROM THEIR BUTH HIS TRANSPORTATION TO CAIRO WHERE HE

IS DETAILED WAS ORDERED BY HIGHER QUARTERS ISTANBUL

IS NOW BEING INFORMED BY OUR FRIENDS IN BUDAPEST THAT

EVERYTHING WILL BE LOST UNLESS BRANDT RETURNS AT ONCE FOLLOWINGMY

REPORT THE CONCLUSIONS OF THE EXECUTIVES ARE THAT WHILE THE EXCHANGE

PROPOSITION MAY BE MERE EYE WASH AND THAT THERE IS A POSSIBILITY

OF ULTERIOR MOTIVES IT MUST BE ASSUMED THAT IT IS NOT IMPROBABLE

THAT PRELIMINARY NEGOTIATIONS MIGHT RESULT IN A

SUBSTANTIL NUMBER BEING SAVED. ACCORDING TO INFORMATION

RECEIVED BY US IT WAS AGREED BY EDEN DURING CONVERSATION

WITH WEITZMANN THAT THE POLICY WHOULD BE TO GAIN TIME

TO AVOID THE OTHER SIDE OBTAINING THE IMPRESSION THAT

THE ALLIES ARE SLAMMING THE DOOR AND REFUSING TO EVEN

143

GIVE THE MATTER CONSIDERATION. ALTHOUGH THE HELPFULNESS
OF THIS ATTITUDE IS APPRECIATED IT IS FELT BY US THAT
MORE IS WARRANTED. IT HAS BEEN PROPOSED THAT SEPS
SHOULD BE TAKEN AT ONCE WITH A VIEW TO EXPLORE THE
POSSIBILITY OF MEETING WITH GERMAN REPRESENTATIVES SAY
IN MADRID OR LISBON FOR THE PURPOSE OF DISCUSSING THE
RESCUE OF JEWS URGING AT THE SAME TIME THAT PENDING THE
MEETING DEPORTATIONS AND SLAUGHTER BE DISCONTINUED AT ONCE.

INTERGOVERNMENTAL REFUGEE COMMITTEE WAR REFUGEE
BOARD RED CROSS OR ANY OTHER SUITABLE AGENCY MIGHT BE
THE BODY APPEARING ON BEHALF OF THE ALLIES. IT HAS ALSO
BEEN URGED THAT BRANDT RETURN AT ONCE TO REPORT THAT THE
MESSAGE HAS B   DELIVERED AND THAT ACTIVE CONSIDERATION
IS BEING GIVEN TO IT. I HAVE ALSO REQUESTED URGENT
PRIORITY FOR ME TO FLY TO LONDON. IT IS REQUESTED THAT
YOU ACT IN ACCORDANCE WITH THIS.

A MESSAGE SIMILAR TO THIS HAS BEEN SENT THROUGH THE
BRITISH GOVERNMENT TO WEIZMANN

                              PINKERTON

144

TOD 2318/6/23/4415

CCC V WE 4

TO NAVCOM FOR CCC BY TT

DCR/C NO 801 DATE JUNE 16 1944

TELEGRAM NO 1815 JUNE 13 4 PM FROM ALEGATION LISBON

TO WRB LEAVITT

FOR PILPEL

1815 JUNE 13 4 PM

     PROPOSAL REFERRED TO OUR MAY 4, YOUR MAY 15
CAME FROM JOEL BRANK FROM HUNGARY VISITOR MAYERS.
BRANK JUST VISITED RESNIK ISTANBUL AND PRESUMABLY
NOW TALKING JEWISH AGENCY PALESTINE. SALY KNOWS
OF THESE TRAVELS OF BRANDS AND THINKS BRANK OFFICIALLY
REPRESENTS JEWISH COMMUNITIES HUNGARY AND SLOVAKIA
POSSIBLE ALSO ROUMANIA. THIS FROM LEAVITT FROM PILPEL
WRB 14 WRB 88. SALY THINKS BRAND RELIABLE. COMMENT
AFTER WAR NOT POSSIBLE.

     UNION RTHODOX RABBIS UNITED STATES CANADA ASKED
FOR HIGH SUM THIS PURPOSE BY RABBI JOSEPH STERNBUSCH
IN BEHALF RABBI FREUDIGER HUNGARY. BRAND FREUDIGER
MEMBERS SAME COMMITTEE BUT UNABLE COMBINE EFFORTS.
SCHWARTZ HAS ALL INFORMATION. WRB SWITZERLAND KNOWS OF REFERENCE
TO WASHINGTON OF FREUDIGER-STERNBUSCH
PROPOSITION. STERNBUSCH WAITING FOR ANSWER.
(SIGNED) NORWEB.

TOD 1913 16 JUNE 44 OL...

RECD IN 4 CCC TOD 1913 JUNE 44

145

Dear Mr. Price:

I have received your letter of September 9, 1944, concerning three messages which you are holding relating to certain negotiations with the Gestapo with respect to the release of refugees from enemy territory.

While I appreciate your concern over the nature of these messages, I wish to advise you that they deal with matters in which the Board is deeply interested and which we are following very closely. Should the messages be released by Censorship, I assure you that their texts will not be given to the private organization to which they are addressed. They will be used by the Board solely as a basis for discussion with representatives of the organization.

With respect to the question of Foreign Funds Control licenses, the Board has consulted the Treasury and has been advised that insofar as licenses are required, these messages are deemed to be licensed.

Very truly yours,

(Signed J. W. Pehle

J. W. Pehle
Executive Director

Mr. Byron Price,
Director,
The Office of Censorship,
Washington, D. C.

*Original signed by
mr. Pehle*

146

*Cleared
with Warren.*

FH:agr 9-14-44

DEPARTMENT
OF
STATE

INCOMING
TELEGRAM

DIVISION OF
COMMUNICATIONS
AND RECORDS

FMH-116
Distribution of true
reading only by special
arrangement ▆▆▆▆ W)

Stockholm

Dated September 11, 1944

Rec'd 3:10 a.m., 12th

Secretary of State,

Washington.

CONTROL COPY

DEPARTMENT OF STATE
DIVISION OF
SEP 12 1944
COMMUNICATIONS
AND RECORDS

3565, September 11, 10 p.m.

German group mentioned in our number 41, 43 and 52
for WRB (Legation's 2362 of June 28, 10 p.m.; 2419 July
3, noon and 2621 of July 15, 10 a.m.) have recently
renewed their approaches with respect to freeing Baltic
Jews against 2,000,000 Swedish kronor of civilian relief
supplies for German bombed-out population and a concrete
proposal allegedly will be advanced this week with Berlin
approval. In the meantime it is stated the German
authorities have issued strict orders to stop further
Jewish persecutions in the Baltic countries.

We are also advised that Boening returned to
Germany for military service but was immediately
released and sent to Bern. It is possible that he is
involved in some of the German negotiations in Switzerland with respect to Jews, particularly Hungarian.
Believe it highly desirable that there be a close interchange of information as to any such negotiations. This
is our number 80 for WRB.

JOHNSON

JMS

See: German Proposals Thru Sweden

Doc. 26

147

Miss Hodel —

Control copy went to Lesser.

He requested that no
distribution be made
until you returned.

RD

All of Olsen's references are in your
Sweden (10) file.

148

ORIGINAL TEXT OF TELEGRAM SENT

FROM: Secretary of State, Washington

TO: American Legation, Bern

DATE: September 12, 1944

NUMBER: 3153

CONTROL COPY

For McClelland from Department and War Refugee Board.

Please report at once on Saly Mayer negotiations of September 4 and 5.

For your information, Ambassador Norweb has cabled that Hungarian Charge d'Affaires, Lisbon, states he has received telegram from his Government dated September 3, substance of which is as follows:

His Government has no knowledge of and no part in any conversations which the Gestapo with or without representatives of the Hungarian Jewish community is carrying on with any other persons private or official or with any allied body. All deportations from Hungary were stopped completely some weeks ago and no incident concerning Jews has occurred in Hungary since the beginning of August when an incident caused by an inferior Gestapo agent was sharply complained about by the Hungarian Government. The Government takes the position that it absolutely excludes any interference in Hungarian Jewish affairs by any German authority.

This is WRB cable to Bern No. 166.

HULL

Doc. 27

149

DEPARTMENT
OF
STATE

INCOMING
TELEGRAM

DIVISION OF
COMMUNICATIONS
AND RECORDS

War Ref Bd Con Betts

NMC-75
Distribution of true
reading only by special
arrangement. ▮▮▮▮ W)

Lisbon

Dated September 14, 1944

Rec'd 9:44 p.m.

CONTROL COPY

Secretary of State,

Washington.

2881, September 14, 7 p.m.

WRB 194 FOR LEAVITT FROM PILPEL JDG 73.

Advice from Mayer is that period of delay ends

mid-night fourteenth.

NORWEB

Doc. 28

150

JT

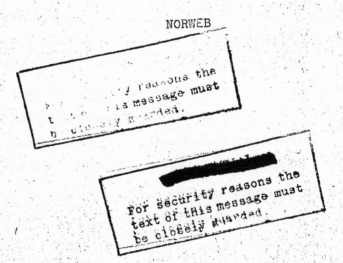

...y reasons the
...is message must
...rded.

For security reasons the
text of this message must
be closely guarded.

INCOMING
TELEGRAM

PLAIN

Lisbon

Dated September 14, 1944

Rec'd 12:40 p.m. 15th.

Secretary of State,

Washington.

2884, September 14, 7 p.m.

FOR LEAVITT FROM ROBERT PILPEL WRB 192 JDC 74.

View terrible responsibilities which Salymayer

courageously carrying believe message from you would

be appreciated.

NORWEB

RR

CONTROL COPY

Doc. 29

151

PARAPHRASE OF TELEGRAM RECEIVED

FROM: American Legation, Bern

TO: Secretary of State, Washington

DATED: September 15, 1944

NUMBER: 6092

Reference is made herewith to Department's cable of August 23,
No. 2900, WRB 129.

There follows a summary of the material portion of the
Swiss note of September 13 which states that report from the
Swiss Legation in Budapest indicates that it has followed the
development of the situation of Budapest Jews in order various
questions which the Department presented:

It is currently established that the Hungarian Government,
under German pressure, has decided on transfer of Jewish residents
of Budapest to Hungarian provinces and that this is to occur in
the immediate future.

After assembly Jews of both sexes from 14 to 70 years of
age must be incorporated in the Hungarian labor service while
persons above and below these age limits must be concentrated
in provincial camps.

It seems that the Hungarian Government is to O.K. these
measures to protect Jews against whom the German Government for
its part, without consulting Hungarian authorities, would otherwise have taken measures.

HARRISON

DCR:VAG:MFR   9/13/44

Doc. 30

152

Distribution of true reading only by special arrangement. (SECRET W)

War Refugee Board

AMEMBASSY,

LISBON

2532

The following for Norweb is WRB 87.

Reference is made to your 2873 of August 30. Discussions referred to therein are taking place with knowledge of Department and WRB, who are being kept advised by Amlegation Bern.

HULL
(MMV)

CONTROL COPY

Doc. 31

153

WRB:MMV:OMH   WE
9/15/44

FROM: American Legation, Bern

TO: Secretary of State, Washington

DATED: September 16, 1944

NUMBER: 6110

CONTROL COPY

~~CONFIDENTIAL~~

McClelland sends the following for the War Refugee Board.

Reference is made in the following to the Legation's July 24 cable No. 4729; and its August 26 cable No. 5588 and the Department's September 12 cable No. 3153.

Discussions with the Gestapo were continued by Saly Mayer (SM) on September 3, 4, and 5 at St. Margarethen. Only one man from the German side (member of SS) was present accompanied by Wilhelm Bielitz and Kasztner. As instructed, SM did not negotiate in name of JDC but only in the name of a private Swiss Jewish organization. For SM these prolonged discussions devoted to gaining time without making any commitments, were exceedingly difficult and trying, as he could tell the Germans only that the matter had been referred to "higher quarters" and that an answer was awaited daily. Meanwhile he invited the Nazis to present a detailed list of goods they desired and which might be found in Switzerland. Figures as high as one hundred million Swiss francs were talked of by the Nazis and they declared they would have to

come

Doc. 32

154

come to Switzerland for a stay of some days in order to
compile exact list. Swiss authorities have been very
reluctant to grant even temporary entry permits for such
a purpose to present date.

My personal opinion and that of SM also, is that all
time possible has now been gained and that in all probability
the Gestapo has lost patience so that these negotiations
can be considered as having lapsed which after all were
ultimately doomed to failure.

Actually SM negotiations did not primarily concern
Jews still in Hungary but rather those still alive and
deported outside of Hungary into territory occupied by the
Germans.

155

HARRISON

DCR:EBH:EFR   9/18/44

ORIGINAL TEXT OF TELEGRAM SENT

FROM: Secretary of State, Washington

TO: American Legation, Bern

DATED: September 16, 1944

NUMBER: 3196

CONTROL COPY

CABLE TO MINISTER HARRISON AND MCCLELLAND.

The following is the substance of a communication received from Minister Johnson and Olsen in Stockholm:

QUOTE A German group consisting of Boening, Kleist and Klause have recently renewed their approaches with respect to freeing Baltic Jews against 2,000,000 Swedish kronor of civilian relief supplies for German bombed-out population and a concrete proposal allegedly will be advanced this week with Berlin approval. In the meantime it is stated the German authorities have issued strict orders to stop further Jewish persecutions in the Baltic countries.

We are also advised that Boening returned to Germany for military service but was immediately released and sent to Bern. It is possible that he is involved in some of the German negotiations in Switzerland with respect to Jews, particularly Hungarian. Believe it highly desirable that there be a close interchange of information as to any such negotiations. UNQUOTE

THIS IS WRB CABLE TO BERN NO. 172.

HULL

RECEIVED

Doc. 33

156

copy

DSH-507
This telegram must be
paraphrased before being
communicated to anyone
other than a Government
Agency. (SECRET-O)

Bern

Dated October 5, 1944

Rec'd 2:10 p.m.

Secretary of State,

Washington.

For security reasons the
text of this message must
be closely guarded.

6619, October 5, 8 a.m.

FOR WRB FROM MCCLELLAND.

I have received a number of reports lately dealing
with most recent developments in situation of Jews in
Slovakia and Hungary of which I consider following
pertinent details would interest you.

Report from Bratislava dated September 27 states
that due to cooperation of various Jewish youth groups
with Partisan Gestapo has instigated general concentration of all Jews in provinces. They are being mainly
assembled at camp of Sered which was taken earlier in
month by Partisans. About 500 Jews were liberated (but
later recaptured by Germans. Germans are also said to
be concentrating Jews at Trencsin. About 1700 Jewish
internees from camp at Novaky were recently liberated
by Partisans who still control this region. All Jews
capable of bearing arms from Novaky have been enrolled
in resistance units.

According to

DECLASSIFIED
State Dept. Letter, 1-11-72
By R. H. Perks Date SEP 27 1972

Doc. 34

157

-2-, #6619, October 5, 8 a.m., from Bern.

According to report from Czech resistance operating in Slovakia dated September 19 Tito declared he had received "assurances" from Germans that Jews in provinces were simply being concentrated but would "not be removed from Slovak territory". This can scarcely be relied upon and telegram from responsible Jewish circles in Bratislava dated October 3 indicates that deportations from provinces (scale unknown) are already taking place.

Situation in Bratislava itself while tense appears quiet as far as deportations are concerned and central Jewish office under direction Mrs. Fleischmann continues to function. Rescue activity now consists mainly in procuring false "Aryan" papers for and in hiding Jews. There is a certain volume of flight back to Hungary.

I sent a further sum of 100,000 Swiss francs from WRB funds to support all such practical rescue activities with Coujier who left October 4 for Bratislava and Budapest.

During his most recent interview with Kasztner, Biolitz and a new Gestapo agent at Swiss German frontier on September 29 Saly Mayer elicited unwilling assurances from German that no deportations from Slovakia would

take place

-3-, #6619, October 5, 8 a.m., from Bern.

take place as long as "negotiations" continued. This
seems to have been successful to date in any event as
far as Jews in Bratislava are concerned.

Status of Mayer's negotiations with Germans remains very much as reported in Legation's 6110,
September 16. Claiming that he did not have necessary
technical qualifications for compiling list of goods
Germans desired in Switzerland, Mayer again invited
them to send representatives for this purpose here.
It is however still most doubtful that Swiss authorities
will grant such visas, as presence Gestapo men Switzerland is highly distastful to them. I have discussed
matter informally with Swiss and Mayer is taking it up
once more this week. By bluffing it has happily been
possible to draw matters out another time although
whole affair is becoming very strained.

During this recent interview Kasztner reported
that as yet no movement of Jews out of Budapest (Loga-
tion's 6447, September 28) had begun. However notorious
SS "obersturmbann Fuehrer" Eichmann formerly of Lublic
who along with his henchman "Hauprsturm Fuehrer"
Wisliceny was responsible from German side for organization of mass deportation of Jews from Hungary in

May and June

159

-4-, #6619, October 5, 8 a.m., from Bern.

May and June has been transferred back to Budapest from Temesvar. His return at this time is most disquieting sign.

Another report from Budapest dated September 13 received through representative of Hungarian resistance movement in Zurich indicates that it was possible during July and August (Legation's 4394, July 11) to organize evacuation of some 7,000 Jewish men including the families of 400 from southern Hungary to partisan controlled Yugoslav territory. Men capable bearing arms have been enrolled Partisan forces those physically unsuited, women and children have been moved to interior but are living under extremely primitive conditions. In attempt alleviate this shipment have recently financed shipment of medical and sanitary supplies for these refugees.

                              HARRISON

MEV

160

INCOMING
TELEGRAM

DEPARTMENT OF STATE
DIVISION OF

DIVISION OF
COMMUNICATIONS
AND RECORDS

MB-976

Lisbon

Distribution of true
reading only by special
arrangement. (W)

1944 OCT 11 PM 2 14

Dated October 10, 1944

COMMUNICATIONS
AND RECORDS
(LIAISON)

Rec'd 4:27 p.m.

Secretary of State,

Washington.

CONTROL COPY

3102, October 10, 6 p.m.

FOR LEAVITT FROM ROBERT PILPEL

This is WRB 215 JDC 85.

Kastner and another Jewish member of the
delegation will visit Saly within a few days. Saly
requests you authorize him to talk to delegation in
terms of 20,000,000 Swiss francs. All he requires is
possession of a document showing he is authorized to
that extent.

NORWEB

JMS
WMB

Doc. 35

161

THE OFFICE OF CENSORSHIP
WASHINGTON 25

BYRON PRICE
DIRECTOR

BY MESSENGER

October 17, 1944.

REVISED
E. O. 11652, Sec. 3(E) and 5(D) or (E)
FDA Ltr 12/19/75
By SLR   Date JAN 16 1976

Mr. John W. Pehle,
Executive Director,
War Refugee Board,
Washington, 25, D. C.

Dear Mr. Pehle:

It was unfortunately not practicable to answer your letter of September 15 until receipt of the views of the Department of State. I assume that your office has now received a copy of Secretary Hull's letter dated October 9.

I feel that the Office of Censorship is in duty bound to suppress the three messages referred to in my letter of September 9. This action is predicated upon the following circumstances which, in our opinion, seem to be established beyond a reasonable doubt:

Doc. 36

162

(a) Even though Mr. Mayer may be a Swiss citizen, he is, in the last analysis of this correspondence, acting as an agent of the Joint Distribution Committee.

(b) It is apparently the object of this negotiation to transfer twenty-five million dollars of private American funds to Switzerland.

(c) It seems clear that after some involved transactions the ultimate disposition of these funds will benefit the Gestapo in the nature of a ransom payment.

(d) It would appear that transactions of this nature are clearly in violation of the "Trading with the Enemy Act" on the part of the Joint Distribution Committee.

(e) The Office of Censorship, like other agencies and departments of the government, is obliged to observe and enforce the policies of the United States Government.

I am sure you will understand that the Office of Censorship is not prepared to be a party to transactions in the nature of ransom payments, unless it can be established that such transactions are in conformity with the stated policy of the government. The correspondence includes no such commitment or statement of policy.

Relative to your statement that the messages "will be used by the Board solely as a basis for discussion with representatives of the organization," it is difficult to see how these messages can be discussed without practical disclosure of their content and purpose. No such use of these messages is approved, as such would be equivalent to the virtual delivery of a suppressed message.

Sincerely yours,

Byron Price,
Director.

2 Cow Rf Bd-Pehle

FROM: Secretary of State, Washington

TO: American Embassy, Moscow

DATED: October 20, 1944   **CONTROL COPY**

NUMBER: .   2484

AMBASSADOR HARRIMAN, MOSCOW, FROM WAR REFUGEE BOARD.

Kindly refer to Department's 1812 of July 28. — _Joel Brandt Proposal — (Secret)_

The Department considers it desirable to inform the Soviet Government of the following. The Department has been advised that discussions have recently taken place on the Swiss border between representatives of the Jewish groups in Budapest, accompanied by reputed Gestapo agents, and Swiss citizens representing the Swiss Jewish community in an effort by the latter group to forestall, if at all possible, the continued deportation and extermination particularly of Jews from Hungary and Slovakia. The Swiss citizens involved in these discussions have acted in the belief that lives can be saved and precious time gained by prolonging discussion pending the solution of the problem by military action. No commitments or agreements have been made or authorized. The discussions are currently being reported to American Jewish groups and any significant developments will be reported to Moscow.

HULL

Doc. 37

163

ORIGINAL TEXT OF TELEGRAM SENT

FROM: Secretary of State, Washington

TO: American Legation, Bern

DATED: October 20, 1944

NUMBER: 3578

Doc. 38

164

TO MINISTER HARRISON AND MCCLELLAND FROM WAR REFUGEE BOARD.

In response to recent requests of Saly Mayer through Pilpel in Lisbon for credit of 20,000,000 Swiss francs, we have been advised by the Joint Distribution Committee that they have authorized this amount in substitution for the amount referred to in Department's 2990, WRB's 153 of August 30. No commitment to make any payment from this amount can be entered into without approval here. Mayer should be fully advised of all the foregoing.

THIS IS WRB BERN CABLE NO. 227.

HULL

20 OCT 23 AM 11 05

WASHINGTON D C
WAR REFUGEE BOARD
RECEIVED

CABLE TO MINISTER HARRISON, BERN, FROM WAR REFUGEE BOARD.

Please deliver the following message to Saly Mayer, Bern,
Switzerland, from the American Jewish Joint Distribution
Committee:

    QUOTE JOINT DISTRIBUTION COMMITTEE HEREBY AUTHORIZES
    YOU TO CARRY ON NEGOTIATIONS ON BASIS 20,000,000 SWISS
    FRANCS UNQUOTE

The amount herein specified is in substitution for the
amount specified in Department's 2990, WRB's 153 of August 30.
No commitment to make any such payment can be entered into
without approval here. Mayer should be so advised.

THIS IS WRB CABLE TO BERN NO. 217.   165

3:45 p.m.
October 16, 1944

Miss Chauncey (for the Sec'y) Abrahamson, Cohn, DuBois, Friedman,
Hodel, Lesser, Merks, Mannon, McCormack, Files

JBF:LSL:JWP:dg 10/16/44

Z Pehe (WRB)

ORIGINAL TEXT OF TELEGRAM SENT

FROM: Secretary of State, Washington

TO: American Embassy, London

DATED: October 21, 1944

NUMBER: 8780

CONTROL COPY

FOR WINANT AND MANN, LONDON FROM WAR REFUGEE BOARD. *see: Joel Brandt Proposal*

Kindly refer to Department's 5949 of July 28.

The Department considers it desirable to inform the British Government of the following. The Department has been advised that discussions
have recently taken place on the Swiss border between representatives of
the Jewish groups in Budapest, accompanied by reputed Gestapo agents, and
Swiss citizens representing the Swiss Jewish community in an effort by
the latter group to forestall, if at all possible, the continued deportation and extermination particularly of Jews from Hungary and Slovakia.
The Swiss citizens involved in these discussions have acted in the belief
that lives can be saved and precious time gained by prolonging discussion
pending the solution of the problem by military action. No commitments or
agreements have been made or authorized. The discussions are currently
being reported to American Jewish groups and any significant developments
will be reported to Moscow.

In Department's 2484 of October 20 the foregoing has also been transmitted to Moscow.

STETTINIUS
(Acting)

2 WRB (Pehle)

FROM: American Embassy, Moscow via Army.

TO: Secretary of State, Washington.

DATED: October 23, 1944.

NUMBER: 4041.

CONTROL COPY

Department's message dated October 20, Number 2484, as received here states that there have been conducted discussions by Swiss citizens who are representative of the Swiss community, and information is requested as to whether Swiss Jewish Community is meant by this.

Doc. 40

167

KENNAN.

DCR:LCW

10-24-44

2 War Rf Bd - Pehle

PARAPHRASE OF TELEGRAM SENT

FROM: Secretary of State, Washington

TO: American Embassy, Moscow

DATED: October 27, 1944

NUMBER: 2533
K

CONTROL COPY

With regard to message of October 23, 2 p.m., from the Embassy, Number 4041, UCTE, SWISS JEWISH COMMUNITY, is correct text portion of message of October 20, 7 p.m., from the Department, Number 2484.

STETTINIUS
Acting

168

WRB:MMV:KG

PARAPHRASED: 11-2-44   DCR:LDW

_ARTMENT
OF
STATE

INCOMING
TELEGRAM
DEPARTMENT OF STATE
DIVISION OF

DIVISION OF
COMMUNICATIONS
AND RECORDS

1944 OCT 27 PM 2 07

COMMUNICATIONS
AND RECORDS
(LIAISON)

GEM-265
Distribution of
true reading only by
special arrangement.
(P)

Lisbon

Dated October 26, 1944

Rec'd 10:10 p.m.

Secretary of State,

Washington.

3272, October 26, 10 p.m.

THIS IS JDC 101 WRB 236 FOR LEAVITT FROM PILPEL

Switzerland has authorized visas for delegation

from Hungary which may confer with Saly again. Saly

advises deportations in Hungary underway. Also food

situation serious.

NORWEB

BB

Doc. 41

169

DEPARTMENT OF STATE
DIVISION OF
CORRECTION

1944 OCT 28   AM October 27, 1944

MFD-265
Distribution of
true reading only by
special arrangement.
(SECRET W)

COMMUNICATIONS
AND RECORDS
(LIAISON)

In cable number 3272, October 26, 10 p.m., from Lisbon, code block should be "(SECRET W)" instead of "(SECRET F)".

DIVISION OF COMMUNICATIONS AND RECORDS
JMB

170

For security reasons the text of this message must be closely guarded.

CONTROL COPY

PARAPHRASE OF TELEGRAM RECEIVED

FROM: American Embassy, Moscow

TO: Secretary of State, Washington

DATED: October 31, 1944

NUMBER: 4174

CONTROL COPY

Following is for the attention of the War Refugee Board.

The substance of Department's messages of October 20 and 27, nos. 2484 and 2533 respectively, have been sent by me to the Foreign Office.

Doc. 42

KENNAN

171

DCR:WAG   11/1/44

DEPARTMENT
OF
STATE

INCOMING
TELEGRAM

DIVISION OF
COMMUNICATIONS
AND RECORDS

DEPARTMENT OF STATE
DIVISION OF

EL-160   1944 NOV 6 AM 10 07
This telegram must be
paraphrased before being
communicated to anyone
other than a Government
Agency. (SECRET-ODN)

Bern

Dated November 4, 1944

Rec'd 5:25 p.m.

Secretary of State,

Washington,

7339, November 4, 3 p.m.
        x
FOR WRB FROM MCCLELLAND

Department's 3436, October 6 and 3609, October 23.

Doc. 43

172

   Many thanks for these two wires. Interesting
information contained in them concerning Nazi negotiations
in Sweden has been most valuable and revealing.

   Saly Mayer's negotiations last reported on in
Legation's 6619, October 5, have again reached a
critical and difficult stage with arrival in Switzerland
on November 1, of delegation consisting of Kasztnerbielitz
and two SS men. Although it will be impossible to stall
and bluff much longer this may afford an opportunity to
drive home to Nazis the inevitable fate which awaits them
as result of their continued ruthlessness. Also any seeds
of dissent which can be sown in their ranks will be planted
Their hand as negotiators has been considerably weakened
by recent happenings in Hungary and Slovakia.

                            HARRISON

WFS

DEPARTMENT
OF
STATE

INCOMING
TELEGRAM

DIVISION OF
COMMUNICATIONS
AND RECORDS

JP-884
Distribution of true
reading only by
special arrangement.
(████ W)

Bern

Dated November 16, 1944

Rec'd 10:28 p.m.

For security
text of ██████ the
be clos████ guarded.

CONTROL COPY

Secretary of State

Washington

7565, November 16, 2 p.m.

FOR PEHLE OF WRB FROM MCCLELLAND

Negotiations last referred to our 7339 have been
continued in Switzerland almost daily by Saly Mayer (SM)
since November 1. They have become increasingly strained
and difficult. (Department's 3578, October 20 and
Legation's 7339, November 4).

Kasztner and Bielitz left for Budapest and chief
SS negotiator "Obersturmbann Fuehrer B" for Berlin on
November 6, latter ostensibly to report to Himmler prior
to returning to Budapest. Negotiator B left behind his
henchman K in Switzerland to pursue conversations with
SM.

SM has been negotiating for following conditions:
Two. Verification and control that these terms are carried
out to be exercised by ICRC or other acceptable neutral
and impartial body all necessary permission and facilities
for performance of this duty to be granted by Germans.

One. Cessation

Doc. 44

173

One. Cessation by Germans of all actions which
are not directly related to normally accepted concept
of a war effort that is mistreatment calculated to bring
death execution and outright extermination with respect
to all (repeat all) detainees in German hands regardless
of nationality both Jewish and non-Jewish. Specifically
mentioned: over 100,000 Jews (aged, invalid and children)
remaining in Budapest.

Four. All individual Jews specified by JDC or by
other recognized Jewish organizations through JDC (members
of Bratislava Jewish Office for instance) to be released.

174

Three. All Jews in German hands in Hungary and elsewhere holding documents or passports of belligerent
countries immigration or entry visas to countries neutral
and otherwise outside German controlled territory to be
allowed to leave. Specifically mentioned: case of some
8,000 Jews at Bergen-Belsen.

All information that might subsequently be requested
concerning welfare whereabouts of any other groups of Jews
not specifically mentioned to be supplied.

These stipulations were supposed submitted to Himmler
on or about November 10 by chief SS negotiator B. B has
now returned to Budapest and awaits word from his assistants
still in St. Gall that SM has placed at their disposal
20,000,000 Swiss francs which amount was "authorized" SM

in your 3578

in your 3578 by JDC.

SM has informed K that 20,000,000 can only be put
up as deposit held by neutral third party acceptable to
both sides. K, however, is unwilling to accept credit
(he thinks SM is actually holding money) in this manner
so SM paried by stating that 20,000,000 were "blocked"
pending submission by K of list of goods desired. Meanwhile,
Swiss police hesitate to prolong K's "visa desejour" which
expires November 15 or to allow him freedom of movement elsewhere than in St. Gall. SM is trying tp persuade Swiss
to permit K to travel so that K can draw up precise list of
nature and quantity of goods desired. In midst of this more
or less deadlock situation, SM has urged joint office in
Lisbon to cable JDC, New York, requesting that 20,000,000
francs be transferred to him immediately. He has asked me to
support this request.

I have been able to assure myself personally that Nazis
primary interest in this whole affair is to secure first
sizable amounts of Swiss francs (on arrival in Switzerland
they considered the 20,000,000 comparatively small money) and
secondly exportation of goods to be purchased with these
funds in Switzerland which are of value to German war effort.
SM's attempt to talk them around to considering goods of
non-military value has elicited little or no response. Their

stipulation

175

stipulation is that SM and I will secure permission from Allies for export of goods they select, at least in part, from Switzerland.

In view of fact that original goal of gaining time specifically in relation to situation of Jews in Hungary has been attained, SM's part and fact that even if funds could be sent there, it would ultimately (within 2 or 3 weeks at most) be necessary for our and other Allied Governments to refuse permission for export of goods of value to German war effort for Switzerland (quite apart from French attitude toward such export which is negative) it is my considered opinion that SM should be instructed by WRB and JDC to discontinue negotiations as tactfully as possible. I personally fear that if bluff is carried too far before being broken off Nazis may effect reprisals on Jews out of anger.

As to political aspects of question subordinate Swiss authorities acquainted with matter have been led to believe negotiations concern purchase relief goods in Switzerland for Jews in German camps. Swiss political department however, is aucourant and has expressed itself willing to do all it can within humanitarian limits to assist with transfer of funds if requested to do so by our government.

Time element originally involved in Hungarian situation seems no longer

seems no longer to be so critically present. Schirmer
of ICRC who left Budapest on October 29, reports interviews
with both Wesermayer and Grell of German Legation and with
Vajna Minister of Interior in Szalsy regime. Germans assured
him that outside of 50,000 male Jews already sent to Austria
as labor they would "in due course" allow emigration of
Palestine certificate holders and those possessing special
protecting documents of Sweden, Switzerland and Spain.
Further that Jewish aged invalids and children (over 100,000)
still in houses in Budapest would not be molested. Neither
Wesermayer nor Grell, of course, can be considered as speaking
authoritatively for SS. In view also of increasingly
difficult transportation situation as well as disorganization
existing ranks of Szalasy regime which does not appear capable
of carrying out concerted anti-Jewish program, it is unlikely
that deportation of Jews remaining in Budapest can or will
be effected or that wholesale massacre of Jews "surplace"
is liable to take place is there ore that these negotiations
be terminated with all due credit to SM for a magnificent
and difficult piece of work.

Please expedite instructions.

HARRISON

MJF

177

OUTGOING TELEGRAM

DEPARTMENT OF STATE

DIVISION OF COMMUNICATIONS AND RECORDS

1944 NOV 20 PM 5 08

November 18, 1944

Midnight

AMLEGATION

COMMUNICATIONS AND RECORDS
(LIAISON)

BERN

3932

TO HARRISON AND MCCLELLAND FROM WAR REFUGEE BOARD

Careful consideration has been given to the subject matter of your cable 7565 of November 16. This is WRB Bern cable 285.

The transaction outlined in your cable cannot (repeat not) be supported by the Board in any way and further it is the Board's opinion that no (repeat no) funds from any source should be used to carry out such proposal.

The Board has carefully considered and recognizes the force of your argument concerning bringing the negotiations to a close. In this connection however the Board is confident that you will take into consideration the fact that because of recent military developments each day that can be gained is of increasing importance.

STETTINIUS
(Acting)

CONTROL COPY

WRB:GLW:kg   WE   BC   SE   EE
11/18/44

Doc. 45

178

DEPARTMENT
OF
STATE

OUTGOING
TELEGRAM

DIVISION OF
COMMUNICATIONS
AND RECORDS

Distribution of
true reading only by
special arrangements NOV 22 PM 1 07

November 2?, 1944

Midnight

AMEMBASSY

LONDON

9769

The following for Mann from Pehle is WRB 2?.

Please advise Dr. Joseph Schwartz that JDC
requests him to proceed to Switzerland at once.
In view of urgency please lend every assistance to
Schwartz in obtaining travel and advise date of
his departure.

Doc. 46

179

STETTINIUS
ACTING
(LSIV)

CONTROL COPY

WRB:MMV:KG
11/20/44

OUTGOING
TELEGRAM

JHH
Distribution of true
reading only by special
ar~~~~~~~~~~

November 22, 1944

1944 NOV 27 p.m. 2 54

War
Ref. Bd.
(M. Pehl)

AMLEGATION

BERN
3962

The following for McClelland from War Refugee Board is
WRB 287.

Joseph Schwartz of the JDC will soon arrive in Switzerland
to discuss with you and other interested persons various problems of refugee rescue and relief. We trust that you will give
him the full benefit of your experience and information in the
matter.

We assume you will inform Schwartz, upon his arrival, of
the contents of our No. 3932 of November 18 (WRB 285) in which
the Board stated its opposition to the transaction outlined
in your No. 7555 of November 18. You should indicate to Schwartz
that under no circumstances may he participate in any way in
the negotiations referred to in your No. 7555, which have been
carried on by S.M. as a representative of the Swiss Jewish community.

Doc. 47

180

CONTROL COPY

WRB:MKV:KG
11/22/44

DEPARTMENT
OF
STATE

INCOMING
TELEGRAM

DIVISION OF
COMMUNICATIONS
AND RECORDS

MB-1263

PLAIN

Lisbon

Dated December 4, 1944

Rec'd 1:26 a.m., 5th

DEPARTMENT OF STATE

DEC 5 1944

DIVISION OF
COMMUNICATIONS AND RECORDS

Secretary of State

Washington.

4125, Fourth

x

For Leavitt from Pilpel JDC 129 Saly met Kastner
at Bern and informed him unable prolong negotiations
further except by resigning as president of Swiss
negotiating committee Saly employed this device and
resigned of course he carrying on and Salys representative meeting Kastner again today Kastner within one
hours distance.

CROCKER

FS

Doc. 48

181

DEPARTMENT
OF
STATE

INCOMING
TELEGRAM

DIVISION OF
COMMUNICATIONS
AND RECORDS

CC-11
Distribution of
true reading only by
special arrangement.
~~(W)~~

Bern

Dated December 15, 1944

Rec'd 9:10 p.m.

Secretary of State,

Washington.

8118, December 13, 7 p.m. (SECTION ONE)

FOR PEHLE OF WRB FROM ~~CRELL~~. *Mc Clelland.*

Department's 3939, November 18, WRB'S 285.

Pursuing negotiations last referred to in Bern's
7565 November 16 Saly Mayer in course of my recent
conversations with news representative which took place
at St. Margae then on Swiss German frontier during
first week in December in an effort to get away from
unfruitful commercial tenor of previous negotiations
made following general proposal to Germans: Extermination
of all "Schutzhaeftlinge" particularly Jewish deportees,
in German hands should cease. In return for this
concession, which Becher at Budapest reports is already
observing pending outcome of negotiations on former
"gods" basis, and in response to German claims that
maintenance of several hundred United States and Jews
constitutes severe strain on their resources Mayer would

procure

For security reasons the text of this message must be closely guarded.

Doc. 49

182

procure the necessary supplies to keep Jews in German
controlled areas alive. The proper distribution of such
supplies would either be effected or at least supervised
by ICRC.

It is significant to note that SS representative a
new man named Crell sent to border by Becher did not
reject Mayer's proposal "prima facie" but agreed to
submit it to his superior and zuoh *even* supported. Fact that
Becher and Shaver attained sufficient interest in these
negotiations to dispatch Crell to talk to Mayer in attempt
to learn why negotiations had "bogged down" after relative
failure of Kettlitz mission (his Swiss visa expired and
he had to leave country at end of November) is also
noteworthy.

Although I am personally skeptical that such a
watered down proposal (from SS view point) will hold any
great interest for Germans certainly nothing has been lost
in making it and a few more precious days have been gained.

HUDDLE

WSB

183

DEPARTMENT
OF
STATE

INCOMING
TELEGRAM

DIVISION OF
COMMUNICATIONS
AND RECORDS

DEPARTMENT OF STATE
DIVISION OF

GEM-1944   Bern
Distribution of 1944 DEC 15   AM 9 59
true reading only by   Dated December 13, 1944
special arrangement.
(____ W)   COMMUNICATIONS   Rec'd 5:19 p.m.
                AND RECORDS
                  (LIAISON)

Secretary of State,

Washington.

8118, December 13, 7 p.m. (SECTION TWO)

It is, however, essential to favorable continuation

of negotiations that Mayer know as soon as possible

whether if Germans should accept this new proposition

the credit of twenty million Swiss francs referred to

in Department's 3578, October 20, WRB's 27 will be made

available to him or if not in cash its equivalent in food-

stuffs, clothing, shoes and medicines.

Mayer will undertake to persuade Germans to shift

over to this new basis, that is allow Jews in their hands

to be supported from outside and firmly believes that

something may come of it.

On a purely realistic basis main advantages apparent

to me such a proposal might for Nazis would be to relieve

them of responsibility of maintaining considerable number

of Jews (one which they can hardly be said have adequately

discharged in past) and possibly afford certain of them

                         opportunity to

184

-2-#8118, December 13, 7 p.m. (SECTION TWO) from Bern.

opportunity to claim preferential treatment from Allies
after war for "humanitarian acts". Implementation of
such a proposal if accepted could give rise to difficult
question for instance whether Nazis could continue to
use such Jews fed and clothed from outside as forced
labor in support of German war effort.

I recommend, however, this new proposal of Mayer's
to serious consideration of Board and hope that all possible support can be given to this most laudable effort
on his part to bring negotiations around to an acceptable
basis.

Your early answer would be appreciated.

(END OF MESSAGE).

HUDDLE

BB

185

CONTROL COPY

AMLEGATION,

BERN

4275

The following for McClelland is WRB 328.

Please refer to your No. 8118 of December 13, 1944. We have read with great interest your comments concerning the new turn which the negotiations have taken. We appreciate Mayer's courage and ingenuity.

As we understand it, the proposal is to furnish, from Switzerland, under appropriate supervision, relief to Jews in German-controlled territory. It is impossible, however, to determine from your cable the exact details of Mayer's proposal. In particular we have no way of knowing whether necessary supplies could be obtained in Switzerland. Nor are we able to determine whether adequate controls could be established through the ICRC or otherwise to assure that the supplies would benefit the Jews and not the Germans. Accordingly it is obviously not possible at this point to determine whether the proposal can be approved. In any event the agreement of the principal Allies would presumably have to be obtained. If a satisfactory scheme can be worked out we feel sure that adequate funds will be available. You are authorized to advise Mayer accordingly.

We will appreciate being fully advised of the progress of these negotiations.

WRB:GLW:OMH   WE   BC   STETTINIUS   SE   EE   CE
12/19/44

Doc. 50

186

For security reasons the text of this message must be closely guarded.

Fran Perel December 20, 1944.

FOR LEAVITT FROM SCHWARTZ.

I have followed very scrupulously instructions not to take part in any discussions which Saly Mayer is conducting. However, I want to associate myself with McClelland's recommendation since that recommendation essentially involves extension of activities already in process through Intercross. Furthermore, I regard latest suggestion which has some possibility of being accepted as face-saving proposal or device which offers possibilities or potentialities of further rescue. In this connection discussions involve 80,000 in Budapest, 17,000 in Vienna, unknown thousands on foot toward Austria, and those in camps in German-occupied Europe, including Belsenbergen. I think highest tribute should be paid to Saly Mayer. Negotiations have gained time and were directly responsible for what happened to Hungarian group from Belsenbergen. However, Saly Mayer's situation will become untenable unless favorable reply to this latest proposal is received. I have complete confidence that all our interests will be protected, both financial and American.

Doc. 51

187

Dear Colonel Gerhardt:

Pursuant to our conversation, I am sending you herewith copies of all of the cables relating to the special negotiations which have been taking place in Switzerland. If you have any further questions concerning this matter, will you please let me know.

Very truly yours,

(Signed) J.W. Pehle

Doc. 52

188

J. W. Pehle
Executive Director

Colonel Harrison A. Gerhardt,
Executive to the Assistant
 Secretary of War,
Room 4E886,
Pentagon Building,
Washington, D. C.

Enclosures.

Sent to Col Gerhardt by
Special messenger - 5:00 PM - 12/27

Initialed copy not
received in file

FH:hd 12/26/44

DEPARTMENT
OF
STATE

INCOMING
TELEGRAM

DIVISION OF
COMMUNICATIONS
AND RECORDS

RS-1884
Distribution of true
reading only by special
arrangement. (SECRET W)

Bern

Dated December 28, 1944

Rec'd 6:24 p.m.

CONTROL COPY

Secretary of State

Washington

8390, December 28, 6 p.m.

FOR PEHLE OF WRB FROM MCCLELLAND

Department's 4273, December 19 WRB's 328 and Legation's 8118, December 13 .

Doc. 53

189

I have discussed exhaustively with Saly Mayer and Joseph Schwartz present status of negotiations as reported in our 8118, in light of your reply, 4273. We reached conclusions that it is indispensable to satisfactory continuation of negotiations that the twenty million Swiss francs be transferred to us as soon as possible so that he may have something tangible to talk with.

Schwartz informs me that this sum will be forthcoming in the United States of America from Jewish sources if its remittance is approved by the competent authorities.

The twenty million should naturally be sent on condition that they can only be spent under proper control by the ICRC for

by the ICRC for maintenance relief and emigration of
Jews in German hands.

His proposal was made to Germans purely in principle,
details as to source of relief goods, their quantity and
shipping rhythm mechanism of ICRC control and similar
questions being purposely left in abeyance so that their
later elaboration might constitute a time-gaining device.

Schwartz is of opinion that there should be no rush
about spending this money once here; and so much the
better if supplies are difficult to find. On other hand
if proposal is accepted by Germans and does reach point
where supplies must be shipped twenty million francs
worth of appropriate relief goods can certainly not
(repeat not) be found in Switzerland. Such essential
items as fats, clothing and shoes are well nigh un-
purchasable here in necessary quantities. On a show-
down supplies would therefore have to come from overseas.

HUDDLE

BB

190

.MENT
OF
STATE

INCOMING
TELEGRAM

DIVISION OF
COMMUNICATIONS
AND RECORDS

CC-1901
Distribution of true
reading only by special
arrangement. (~~STGB W~~ W)

Bern

Dated December 28, 1944

Rec'd 6:44 p.m.

Secretary of State,

Washington.

8390, December 28, 6 p.m. (SECTION TWO)

It has been SM'S main object to bring these

negotiations around to an acceptable basis which could

be freely submitted to our Government our Allies and

to neutral Governments such as Switzerland and Sweden

and even be of a nature to list support and aid of all.

I, therefore, recommend that basic proposal be discussed

with our principal Allies and their agreement in principle

obtained if possible.

If SM can be provided with the twenty million this

will permit them to ask Crell or even Becher to come to

Switzerland once more for further discussion and avoid

breaking off negotiations by default. It will then become

apparent whether Germans are willing to accept SM'S new

proposal in principle.

In light of past few months experience of these

frequent conversations with these I distinctly feel they

are worthwhile continuing as something further may come

of them.

191

-2-#8390, December 28, 6 p.m. (SECTION TWO) from Bern

of them. The recent delivery to Switzerland of Hungarian group from Bergenbelsenrein forces this feeling.

Kindly inform me soon as possible whether the twenty million can be transferred. (END OF MESSAGE.)

HUDDLE

EH

192

MEMORANDUM FOR SECRETARY STETTINIUS

As you know, a series of meetings have been held on the Swiss-German frontier since late August between Saly Mayer, a Swiss citizen, and members of the German Gestapo and SS. Saly Mayer is negotiating for the lives of the Jews still remaining in Nazi-controlled Europe. The discussions have now reached a point where Mayer appears to have succeeded in swinging the negotiations away from ransom to a consideration of a proposal whereby, in return for the halting of the extermination of the Jews in German hands, Saly Mayer would undertake to send to German-occupied countries the necessary relief supplies to keep these Jews alive, provided that the supplies are distributed under International Red Cross supervision.

This proposal, which very significantly the Gestapo and SS negotiators consented to submit to their superiors, was purposely made vague in order that more valuable time might be obtained for clarification of the terms. However, Saly Mayer has concluded that in order to hold open the negotiations, he must have something tangible with which to bait the Nazis and he has requested the transfer of 20,000,000 Swiss francs from the United States to him in Switzerland. The Board's representative in Switzerland, Roswell McClelland, has strongly recommended that we approve such a transfer. It is assumed that the American Jewish Joint Distribution Committee will supply the funds requested.

It is recommended that, for the sole purpose of enabling Saly Mayer to continue these negotiations and to gain more precious time, this Government authorize the transfer of a special fund of 20,000,000 Swiss francs by the American Jewish Joint Distribution Committee to Saly Mayer under the condition that no part of the fund be expended or committed for expenditure without the express

Doc. 54

193

prior approval of this Government. I attach for your
consideration a proposed cable to Bern approving the
transfer and cables to London and Moscow informing them

Department   of such action. These cables have been cleared with the Treasur
~~Secretary Morgenthau~~, but have not been cleared with the
War Department. If you are in agreement, I shall be
pleased to discuss the matter with the War Department.

In view of the extreme urgency of the matter, I
would appreciate an early expression of your views.

(Signed) J.W. Pehle

J. W. Pehle
Executive Director

194   Attachments.

FH:hd 1/3/45

January 6, 1945.

<u>MEMORANDUM FOR THE FILES</u>

Mr. George Warren telephoned me today to advise that the cables to London, Moscow and Bern had been cleared throughout the State Department and would be dispatched about noon today.

Mr. Pehle telephoned Colonel Gerhardt to advise him what had happened and arranged to send Colonel Gerhardt copies of the memorandum to Secretary Stettinius and the three cables.

F. Hodel

DEPARTMENT
OF
STATE
PSH
Distribution of true
reading only by special
arrangement. (SECRET-W)

OUTGOING
TELEGRAM January 6, 1945
DEPARTMENT OF STATE
DIVISION 5 p.m.

1945 JAN 8 PM 2 11

DIVISION OF
COMMUNICATIONS
AND RECORDS

CONFIDENTIAL
COMMUNICATIONS
AND RECORDS
(LIAISON)
For security reasons the
text of this message must
be closely guarded.

CONTROL COPY

AMLEGATION

    BERN

    102
   x

FOR MCCLELLAND FROM DEPARTMENT AND WAR REFUGEE BOARD.

Reference your No. 8390 of December 28, 1944.

This Government is authorizing the remittance of a special
fund of twenty million Swiss francs by the American Jewish Joint
Distribution Committee to Saly Mayer upon condition that no
(repeat no) part of the fund may be expended or committed for
expenditure without the express prior approval of this Government.
The War Refugee Board is relying on you to take such steps as are
necessary to see that this condition is carried out (and you should
report by cable the steps taken.) Presumably, none of these funds
could in any event be paid out without prior approval of our
principal allies. The transfer has been approved solely in order
that Saly Mayer may have something tangible with which to hold
open the negotiations and for the gaining of more precious time.

The British and Russian Governments are being advised that
the above-mentioned transfer of twenty million Swiss francs has
been authorized under the condition specified.

Please keep Department and Board advised of any significant
developments.

                                    STETTINIUS
WRB:GLW:KG   (GTW)
1/5/45   BC   EE   SE   WE   CE

Doc. 56

196

ORIGINAL TEXT OF TELEGRAM SENT

FROM: Secretary of State, Washington

TO: American Embassy, Moscow

DATED: January 6, 1945   **CONTROL COPY**

NUMBER: 35
          x

From Department and War Refugee Board for attention of Harriman.

You are requested to inform the Soviet Government that the discussions referred to in Department's No. 2484 of October 20, 1944, have been continuing and have recently reached a stage where in order to have something tangible with which to prolong the negotiations and thus gain more precious time, the representatives of the Swiss Jewish Community conducting the negotiations requested the transfer to Switzerland of twenty million Swiss francs from private American Jewish sources. This Government has just authorized the American Jewish Joint Distribution Committee to transfer the sum of twenty million Swiss francs to Switzerland upon condition that no part of the fund will be expended or committed for expenditure without the express prior approval of this Government.

You will be kept fully advised of any further significant developments.

STETTINIUS

DEPARTMENT of trut)
reading only by special
agreement. (Smart-W)
STATE

OUTGOING
TELEGRAM
DEPARTMENT OF STATE
DIVISION OF

DIVISION OF
COMMUNICATIONS
4 p.m. AND RECORDS

1945 JAN 8 PM 2 07

AMEMBASSY

COMMUNICATIONS
AND RECORDS
(LIAISON)

LONDON
135

CONTROL COPY
be closely guarded.

TO WINANT AND MANN FROM DEPARTMENT AND WAR REFUGEE BOARD.

You are requested to inform the British Government that the
discussions referred to in Department's No. 8780 of October 21,
1944, have been continuing. The discussions originating in various
ransom proposals have changed in recent weeks to a proposal by the
Swiss participants that in principle, in return for the halting of
the extermination of Jews in German hands, relief supplies might
be made available for distribution under International Red Cross
supervision to keep surviving Jews alive. In order to have something tangible with which to prolong the negotiations and thus
gain more previous time, the representatives of the Swiss Jewish
Community conducting the negotiations have requested the transfer
to Switzerland of twenty million Swiss francs from private American
Jewish sources. This Government has just authorized the American
Jewish Joint Distribution Committee to transfer the sum of twenty
million Swiss francs to Switzerland upon condition that no part of
the fund will be expended or committed for expenditure without the
express prior approval of this Government.

You will be kept fully advised of any further significant
developments.

DECLASSIFIED   The
State Dept. Letter, 1-11-72

By R. H. Parks Date SEP 27 1972

- 2 -

The foregoing has also been transmitted to Moscow.

STETTINIUS
(GEW)

199

WRB:GLW:KG   BC   EE   SE   WE   CE
1/5/48

MEMORANDUM FOR THE FILES

Re: Special Negotiations with the Gestapo
and SS for Saving the Jews of Europe

Background

Following the acceptance by the British and American Governments
of the so-called Horthy offer, the Board was advised on August 11 by
its representative in Switzerland that despite the terms of the Horthy
offer, it now appeared that the emigration of Jews from Hungary would
not be permitted. This was due in large part to the stiffened attitude
of the German Government, which had apparently sent ranking Gestapo
agents of the so-called Sodereinsatz Kommand especially to Budapest
to direct the deportation of the Jews.

After the attack on Hitler and following the rapid deterioration
of the German military situation, the Gestapo in Budapest shifted its
interest from the biological aspects of Jewish extermination to the
purely military benefits in labor, goods and money which could be
derived from the Jews. This attitude was typified by the declaration
of one of the Gestapo chiefs in Budapest to Kasztner, an important
member of the Budapest Jewish Community, to the effect that the Gestapo
now desired to pump out the necessary labor from Hungarian Jewry and
sell the balance of valueless humanity against goods.

On the other hand, the Horthy Government of Hungary, apparently
frightened by world reaction, was striving to make up for the unsavory
role which it had played in the persecution and deportation of the
Jews. It, therefore, favored a solution of the Jewish problem through
emigration and relief under the supervision of the International Red
Cross.

Previous Ransom Proposals

Joel Brandt, a member of the Budapest Jewish Community, was sent
from Budapest to Istanbul, arriving there on May 19, 1944, on the
German courier plane from Vienna, bearing with him a German offer to
halt the deportations and extermination of the Jews in return for 200
tons of tea, 800 tons of coffee, 2 million cakes of soap, and 10,000
trucks "to be used only on the Russian front." After careful consideration, this offer was turned down by the Allied governments and Joel
Brandt was never permitted by the British authorities to return to
Budapest.

Doc. 59

200

In the face of obvious German displeasure because of Brandt's failure to return, an effort was made by Jewish circles in Budapest to keep the negotiations with the Gestapo going by raising goods and valuables from local sources to a value of 3 million Swiss francs and by stating that a credit of 2 million more francs would be obtained in Switzerland to purchase tractors there as well as sheepskins in Slovakia. On the basis of these offers, the Gestapo in Budapest refrained from deporting to Auschwitz during the initial period of deportations, approximately 17,290 Jews. These offers were made as a stopgap in the desperate hope that in the meanwhile, Joel Brandt's negotiations would prove successful and thus render superfluous the other make-shift deals.

Gestapo representatives then expressed a desire to meet in Lisbon with Dr. Joseph Schwartz, chief European representative of the American Jewish Joint Distribution Committee to discuss with him the terms of payment and release of the 17,290 Jews mentioned above who were to be permitted to go to Spain. After the attempt on Hitler's life, the proposed meeting place was changed on orders from Berlin to Irun on the Spanish-French border. Schwartz, an American citizen, was refused permission by the United States Government to meet with the Gestapo representatives.

At this point, the Germans proposed to meet on the Austro-Swiss frontier on or about August 13 with Saly Mayer, a Swiss citizen and the representative in Switzerland of the American Joint Jewish Distribution Committee. As proof of their "good faith," and on the insistence of Kasztner, who later took part in the negotiations, the Germans agreed unconditionally to release a convoy of 500 persons from Bergen-Belsen who were to be permitted to go to Switzerland, and in addition assurances were given that until the negotiations had taken place, no deportations of the 17,290 Jews referred to above would take place.

201

It may also be mentioned by way of background that on July 21, a Gestapo agent had visited certain Jewish groups in Bratislava who had assured him that 300 tractors were available in Switzerland. This news had created a very favorable impression with the Gestapo chief in Budapest, as according to Kasztner, tractors were what the Germans most desired.

In view of the rapidly changing military situation, and in view of the fact that any time gained would operate in favor of the endangered Jews, Roswell D. McClelland, the War Refugee Board representative in Switzerland, recommended that Saly Mayer be permitted to meet with the Gestapo agents on the Swiss-Austrian frontier. After clearance with the State Department, McClelland was advised by the Board that while ransom transactions could not be entered into or authorized by the United States Government, the Board nevertheless had no objection to a meeting taking place between Saly Mayer and the German authorities in order that further time might be gained for the endangered Jews. It was specified by the Board that Saly Mayer could only participate in such discussions as a Swiss citizen and a leader of the Swiss Jewish Community, not as a representative of the American Jewish Joint Distribution Committee or any other American organization.

Saly Mayer Negotiations.

The first meeting between Saly Mayer and the Gestapo and SS representatives took place on August 20, 1944. The Germans advised Saly Mayer that Himmler himself was aware of and approved of the negotiations. They proposed to release all Jews in Nazi controlled territory, including those in Hungary, numbering in all about 1 million, in consideration for the delivery to the German authorities of 10,000 trucks. Saly Mayer replied that any such proposal was bound to meet a categorical refusal from the United States and that furthermore he would not enter into a deal which would involve the delivery of war materials which could be used against the Allies. Saly Mayer suggested that another formula would have to be worked out if the Germans desired to avoid such a refusal. The German representatives stated that the 10,000 truck proposal had originated in Jewish circles in Budapest and had originally been made by Kasztner, not by them. They then suggested a compromise arrangement whereby Saly Mayer would put up a fund of 50 million dollars for the purchase of supplies in neutral countries to be shipped to Germany. Saly Mayer sought and obtained a ten day breathing spell in order that this proposal might be considered.

The second series of meetings between Saly Mayer and the Germans took place on September 3, 4 and 5. This time only one person was present to represent the Germans, a member of the SS. He was accompanied, however, as the last time, by Kasztner and also by Wilhelm Bielitz. In order to stall further for time, Saly Mayer invited the Germans to present a detailed list of the goods they desired. Apparently the Germans were modifying their original demands, for during this meeting the German representative talked in terms of goods valued at 100 million Swiss francs.

On September 29 another meeting took place. This time a new Gestapo agent represented the Germans. As in the former meeting, Kasztner and Bielitz were present. Claiming that he lacked the necessary technical qualifications to compile a list of goods desired in Switzerland, Saly Mayer again invited the Germans to send representatives to Switzerland for that purpose.

202

On October 20, 1944, the War Refugee Board cabled Ambassador Harriman in Moscow requesting him to advise the Russian Government of the discussions that were taking place. The cable to Moscow reads in part as follows:

"The Swiss citizens involved in these discussions have acted in the belief that lives can be saved and precious time gained by prolonging discussion pending the solution of the problem by military action. No commitments or agreements have been made or authorized."

A similar cable was sent by the War Refugee Board to the American Embassy in London on October 21, 1944.

From November 1 to November 16, almost daily meetings were held between Saly Mayer and the Gestapo representatives. Kasztner was present at the earlier meetings. During all this time Saly Mayer ingeniously continued the discussions, making no commitments, keeping the Board's representative fully advised of what was taking place and using every possible device to stall for time.

On November 16 McClelland cabled recommending that Saly Mayer be instructed to discontinue the negotiations as tactfully as possible, as he feared that if the bluff was carried too far before negotiations were broken off, the Nazis might effect reprisals against the Jews. On November 18 the Board replied as follows:

203

"The Board has carefully considered and recognizes the force of your argument concerning bringing the negotiations to a close. In this connection however the Board is confident that you will take into consideration the fact that because of recent military developments each day that can be gained is of increasing importance."

In the meetings with the German representatives which took place at St. Margae on the Swiss-German frontier during the first week in December, Saly Mayer attempted to swing the negotiations away from the fruitless commercial tenor of the former discussions to a consideration of the following general proposal, which it is significant to note was submitted by the SS negotiator, a man named Crell, to his superiors with his support. In return for halting the extermination of the Jews in German control, Saly Mayer would undertake to have sent to Germany the necessary relief supplies to keep these Jews alive, provided that their distribution would be supervised by the International Red Cross. Saly Mayer's proposal was purposely made vague in order that still more valuable time might be obtained pending clarification of the terms.

Thus, no mention was made of the source from which the relief goods would be obtained, the quantities, the timing of the shipments to Germany, the mechanism of control by the International Red Cross, etc.

On December 28, 1944, McClelland cabled that if the negotiations were to be continued any longer it was indispensable that 20,000,000 Swiss francs be transferred to Saly Mayer at once in order that he might have something tangible to talk with. It was pointed out that if matters came to a show-down it would be impossible to obtain that amount of relief supplies in Switzerland, as essential items such as fats, clothing and shoes are almost unobtainable in the necessary quantities, and therefore the supplies would have to come from overseas. However, this problem would furnish a basis for further prolonging the discussions.

After clearance with the State and Treasury Departments, Saly Mayer was advised by cable dated January 6 that the United States Government was authorizing the remittance to Switzerland by the American Jewish Joint Distribution Committee of the Swiss franc equivalent of 5 million dollars upon the condition that no part of this sum would be expended or committed for expenditure without the express prior approval of the United States Government. The War Refugee Board cable to McClelland reads in part as follows:

204

"This transfer has been approved solely in order that Saly Mayer may have something tangible with which to hold open the negotiations and for the gaining of more precious time."

The Russian and British Governments were advised of this new turn in the negotiations in cables sent on the same day.

By way of conclusion it may be mentioned that approximately 1675 Hungarian Jews have been released from concentration camps in German-controlled territory to Switzerland during the course of the Saly Mayer negotiations. Reports to the Board indicate the German negotiators were directly responsible for the release of these Jews.

MEMORANDUM FOR THE FILES

Meeting in Mr. Bernstein's Office, Room 3445
January 24, 1945 at 11:20 A.M.

Present: Messrs. Straessle and Thomen, Swiss Legation
Messrs. Bernstein and Southworth, Treasury

Mr. Straessle reported that a cable had been received indicating approval of the provision of the 20 million Swiss francs for humanitarian purposes which had been requested on January 9, 1945.

In clarification of the arrangements, discussed at the meeting of January 3, 1945, for the purchase by the U. S. Army of certain materials in Switzerland, Mr. Straessle indicated the desire of the Swiss National Bank that the full amount of the payment for these materials bought by the U. S. government should be paid into an account of the Swiss National Bank at the New York Federal and be convertible into freely exportable gold. The Swiss National Bank is to assume the responsibility for conforming to the Swiss export control provisions which relate to the manner in which the exporters are to receive payment, that is, the familiar 50-40-10 percent basis.

In order to provide a basis for the request that the monthly quota of Swiss francs be raised from 8-1/4 million to 12 million, Mr. Bernstein indicated his willingness to transmit to Mr. Straessle a list of the amounts of Swiss francs estimated to be needed by the various government departments in the next six months.

In regard to the application of G.R. 17 to the Swiss bankers, Mr. Straessle indicated his belief that his government would fully meet the wishes of the U. S. government in this matter and he expressed the hope that no action along this line would be taken without prior consultation. Mr. Bernstein agreed to bring this request to the attention of Mr. Schmidt.

S. D. Southworth

Doc. 60

205

SDS:ff 1/25/45

1945 JAN 27 AM 10 42

COMMUNICATIONS AND RECORDS (LIAISON)

CONTROL COPY

US URGENT

AMLEGATION

BERN

420

The following for Huddle and McClelland from Department and War Refugee Board is WRB 382.

Reference Department's No. 102 of January 6, 1945.

You are advised that JDC is making remittance of twenty million Swiss francs this week under license No. W-2402, text of which is as follows:

QUOTE You are hereby authorized, so far as Executive Order No. 8389, as amended, is concerned, and notwithstanding General Ruling No. 11, to remit the sum of Swiss francs 20,000,000 to a banking institution in Switzerland for credit to a joint account in the names of Saly Mayer, President of the Swiss Jewish Refugee Fund, and Roswell D. McClelland, Representative of the War Refugee Board in Switzerland, provided the following terms and conditions shall be complied with:

1. No part of the above sum shall be expended or committed for expenditure except pursuant to a specific United States Treasury license referring to this license.

DECLASSIFIED
State Dept. Letter, 1-11-72
By R. H. Parks Date SEP 27 1972

2. Any

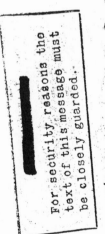

For security reasons the text of this message must be closely guarded.

Doc. 61

206

2. Any withdrawal, transfer, or payment order
    against the above joint account shall be signed
    jointly by Saly Mayer, President of the Swiss
    Jewish Refugee Fund, and Roswell D. McClelland,
    Representative of the War Refugee Board in
    Switzerland.

You, or your bank of account, are authorized to effect
the remittance licensed herein by (a) payment of the dollar
amount involved to the Federal Reserve Bank of New York for
credit to the Banque Nationale Suisse, Zurich, for credit
to the joint account referred to above, or (b) purchase of
the Swiss francs involved from the Federal Reserve Bank of
New York as fiscal agent of the United States, as shall be
prescribed by the Federal Reserve Bank of New York. UNQUOTE

207

                    GREW
                    (Acting)
                    (CLW)

WRB:MMV:KG   WE   SWP
1/25/45

February 16, 1945

Doc. 62

208

General William O'Dwyer
Executive Director
War Refugee Board
Treasury Building
Washington, D. C.

Dear General O'Dwyer:

As you know, we have on deposit in Switzerland the sum of
20,000,000 Swiss francs subject to the signatures of Mr.
Saly Mayer and Mr. Rosswell McClelland.

Subject to the approval of the United States Government,
this sum is available for the purchase of supplies which
can be used to feed Jews in the occupied regions through
the International Red Cross. If proper arrangements can
be made for this purpose, the Joint Distribution Committee
is, of course, glad to have these funds utilized for this
program.

Sincerely yours,

Moses A. Leavitt
Secretary

MAL:RL

AIR MAIL

Bern, April 6th. 1945.

Dear General O'Dwyer:

In one of my early conversations with Herbert
Katzki in Paris he informed me that the Board would
appreciate receiving word from me concerning the claims
wired to the United States by both Mr. Sternbuch of
the Union of Orthodox Rabbis and by the Dutch Jewish
Coordinating Committee of Geneva that Mr. Saly Mayer
of the JDC here in Switzerland had been "sabotaging"
Musy's efforts to bring further groups of Jewish refugees out of Germany to Switzerland.

I was not unaware that Mr. Sternbuch was levelling
such charges against Saly Mayer here but I did not
think that he had gone to the point of cabling them
to his organization in America. With regard to Mr.
Gans of the Dutch Jewish Coordinating Committee I find
it difficult to understand on what grounds he passed
on such erroneous information since neither he nor his
committee have been directly concerned with the Musy
negotiations in Germany. He was therefore peddling
third hand statements.

According to recent talks I have had with Sternbuch
he bases his contention that "Saly Mayer has attempted
to sabotage Musy's efforts" on declarations made by
Musy on the occasion of the latter's return from one of
his trips to Germany some weeks ago. To the best of
my knowledge such an accusation levelled against Saly
Mayer is grossly and flagrantly incorrect. I know Saly
Mayer well and I can unequivocally state that purposely
interfering with Musy's activity in behalf of rescuing
Jewish deportees is the furthest thing from Mr. Mayer's
mind. Saly Mayer has always been the first to applaud
the success of other groups and has never displayed
Musy's tendency to "monopolize" such rescue activities.

It is possible, although we have no way checking
this for certainty, that Kurt Becher, the SS contact
man in Saly Mayer's negotiations, disgruntled by Musy's
initial success, has on his own initiative and in the
interest of maintaining his own prestige attempted in
Berlin to discredit Musy's status as a negotiator in

Doc. 63

209

the matter of the release of Jewish deportees from
Germany. Sternbuch's statement, based on Musy's
claims, that Saly Mayer had collected and supplied
Becher through Kasztner, with all press comment
unfavorable to Musy's negotiations which had appeared
in Switzerland, is not only incorrect but an in-
excusable calumny of Mr. Mayer. If Becher himself
through other channels received such clippings
(which it not impossible) which he displayed in
Berlin, this is purely a question of internal SS
competition and backbiting over which Mr. Mayer has
no control whatever.

Musy and his son returned from Germany on the
afternoon of March 24 (the day before I left for Paris)
empty-handed and with the report that their efforts
to extricate further convoys of deportees had been
unsuccessful. It is my understanding that they have
since returned once more by car to Germany to continue
their negotiations for the release of at least 2000
more people.

210

After Burckhardt's discussions with Kaltenbrunner of the SS, by which negotiations for the
release of large categories of "Schutzhäftlinge"
were more or less officially opened between the
German Government and the International Committee
of the Red Cross, it is not surprising that Musy's
dealings should become of secondary if not less
importance. It is my feeling - and hope - that
ICRC's present negotiations on this broader basis
will now supersede and replace the previous subordinate negotiations carried on through the Saly
Mayer-Becher and Sternbuch-Musy "hook-ups." At the
same time, after a silence of almost 6 weeks during
which time he claimed that he was ill, Becher, who
had been ostensibly at the Grand Hotel in Vienna,
has now announced that he wishes to come at least to
the Swiss frontier to discuss urgent matters with
Saly Mayer. Kasztner will probably accompany Becher.
It is, however, both Saly's and my feeling that since
the fall (or rather near fall at the writing of these
lines) of Vienna and the obvious worsening of Germany's
situation militarily Becher is now interested in a)
trying to sell out certain wealthy Jews belonging to
the Weiss and Chorin families whom the Nazis held as
hostages in Vienna, and b) save his own hide. If this
is the case our bargaining situation will be considerably strengthened and you may be sure we will take
full advantage of it to rescue as many people as
possible.

Very sincerely yours,

Roswell J. McClelland

Brig. General O'Dwyer
War Refugee Board,
Washington, D.C.

CABLE TO AMLEGATION, BERN, FOR MCCLELLAND FROM WAR REFUGEE BOARD

Please deliver the following message to Saly Mayer,
St. Gall, from M. A. Leavitt, American Jewish Joint Distribution Committee:

QUOTE IN ORDER ARRANGE REFUND TWENTY MILLION SWISS
FRANCS PLEASE EXPLAIN TO BANQUE NATIONAL SUISSE WE
RECALLING THIS SPECIAL FUND AND INSTRUCT BANQUE HAVE
DOLLARS FOUR MILLION SIX HUNDRED SIXTY-TWO THOUSAND
FOUR DOLLARS SIXTY-SIX CENTS ($4,662,004.66) EQUIVA-
LENT PAID TO CHASE BANK NEW YORK ACCOUNT AMERICAN
JEWISH JOINT DISTRIBUTION COMMITTEE THROUGH FEDERAL
RESERVE BANK OF NEW YORK. FOR YOUR INFORMATION WAR
REFUGEE BOARD CABLING MCCLELLAND SIMILARLY UNQUOTE

Following is for McClelland from Board.

You are authorized to join Saly Mayer in instructing
Banque Nationale Suisse to pay dollars 4,662,004.66 equivalent to Chase Bank New York account JDC through Federal
Reserve Bank of New York. Fund in question was established
under Treasury license No. W-2402, text of which was sent
you in Department's No. 420 (WRB No. 382) of January 25,
1945. Treasury has approved the ~~transfer~~ ~~back~~ ~~to~~ ~~account~~ recall of fund by
~~of JDC~~ ~~at~~ ~~Chase~~ ~~Bank~~ ~~New~~ ~~York.~~

211

THIS IS WRB BERN CABLE NO. 526

2:10 p.m.
May 19, 1945

Miss Chauncey (for the Sec'y), Cohn, DuBois, Gaston, Hodel, Hutchison,
McCormack, O'Dwyer, Files.

FH:hd 5/18/45 *Cleared with O'Flaherty*
J.J.P.

DEPARTMENT
OF
STATE
~~bution of true
reading only by special
arrangement.   W)

OUTGOING
TELEGRAM

May 23, 194~
4 p.m.

DIVISION OF
CENTRAL SERVICES
TELEGRAPH SECTION

DEPARTMENT OF STATE

MAY 24 1945

CONTROL COPY

AMLEGATION

BERN

1876

The cable below for McClelland is WRB 52~.

Please deliver the following message to Saly Mayer,

St. Gall, from M. A. Leavitt, American Jewish Joint Distribution
Committee:

QUOTE In order arrange refund twenty million Swiss francs
please explain to Banque Nationale Suisse we recalling this
special fund and instruct Banque have dollars four million six
hundred sixty-two thousand four dollars sixty-six cents
($4,662,004.66) equivalent paid to Chase Bank New York account
American Jewish Joint Distribution Committee through Federal
Reserve Bank of New York. For your information War Refugee Board
cabling McClelland similarly. UNQUOTE

Following is for McClelland from Board.

You are authorized to join Saly Mayer in instructing Banque
Nationale Suisse to pay dollars 4,662,004.66 equivalent to Chase
Bank New York account JDC through Federal Reserve Bank of New
York. Fund in question was established under Treasury license
No. W-2402, text of which was sent you in Department's No. 420

(WRB No. 382)

Doc. 64

212

For security reasons the
text of this message must
be closely guarded.

-2-#1876, May 23, 4 p.m., to Bern

(WRB No. 382) of January 25, 1945. Treasury approves recall
of fund by JDC.

GREW
(Acting)
(GLW)

213

WRB:MMV:kg
5/23/45   WL   FM

DEPARTMENT
OF
STATE

INCOMING
TELEGRAM
DIVISION OF
CENTRAL SERVICES

DIVISION OF
CENTRAL SERVICES
TELEGRAPH SECTION

EAS-1514
Distribution of this
reading only by special
arrangement. (SECRET-W)

1945 MAY 28 AM 8:45

Bern

Dated May 26, 1945

Rec'd 6:30 p.m.

DC/L
LIAISON

Secretary of State,

Washington.

CONTROL COPY

2916, May 26, 7 p.m.

WRB FROM MCLELLAND

DEPT'S 1876, WRB's 526, May 23.

According to your instructions the twenty million

Swiss francs held in joint account with Swiss NATL Bank

(SNB) in Saly Mayer's and my names have now been returned

to FEDL Reserve Bank of New York for ACCT of JDC with

Chase NATL. SNB officially confirmed this REF and by

letter May 25.

HARRISON

JT

Doc. 65

214

For security reasons the
text of this message must
be closely guarded.

DEPARTMENT
OF
STATE

INCOMING
TELEGRAM

DIVISION OF
CENTRAL SERVICES
TELEGRAPH SECTION

EF-425

PLAIN

Paris

Dated May 29, 1945

Rec'd 12:57 a.m. 30th

Secretary of State

Washington

3032, Twenty-ninth

FOR WAR REFUGEE BOARD FOR MOSES LEAVITT JOINT
DISTRIBUTION COMMITTEE FROM JOSEPH SCHWARTZ

"Have arranged with McClelland and Saly Mayer for
return of 20 million francs which are intact. Of the
4 million francs which were sent for the account of
McClelland and Sternbusch only 500,000 have been used
for the purchase of food most of which has not been
distributed and we have suggested that the supplies
be turned over to us. Have asked McClelland to return
the balance to New York or turn it over to Saly Mayer.
He advises that in order do this Vaad Hatzalah
New York should cable and write Sternbusch instructing
him to return the funds and to whom. Also suggest
you ask Vaad Hatzalah instruct Sternbusch turn over
distributed supplies to disposal Saly Mayer."

CAFFERY

JMS

Doc. 66

215

In reply please
refer to: 80310

JAN 24 1945

License No. W-2402

Dear Sirs:

You are hereby authorized, so far as Executive Order
No. 8389, as amended, is concerned, and notwithstanding General
Ruling No. 11, to remit the sum of Swiss francs 20,000,000 to a
banking institution in Switzerland for credit to a joint account in
the names of Saly Mayer, President of the Swiss Jewish Refugee Fund,
and Roswell D. McClelland, Representative of the War Refugee Board
in Switzerland, provided the following terms and conditions shall be
complied with:

1. No part of the above sum shall be expended or
committed for expenditure except pursuant to
a specific United States Treasury license
referring to this license.

216

2. Any withdrawal, transfer, or payment order
against the above joint account shall be signed
jointly by Saly Mayer, President of the Swiss
Jewish Refugee Fund, and Roswell D. McClelland,
Representative of the War Refugee Board in
Switzerland.

You, or your bank of account, are authorized to effect the
remittance licensed herein by (a) payment of the dollar amount involved to the Federal Reserve Bank of New York for credit to the
Banque Nationale Suisse, Zurich, for credit to the joint account
referred to above, or (b) purchase of the Swiss francs involved from
the Federal Reserve Bank of New York as fiscal agent of the United
States, as shall be prescribed by the Federal Reserve Bank of New
York.

Sincerely yours,

(Signed) Orvis A. Schmidt

Orvis A. Schmidt
Director

American Jewish Joint Distribution Committee, Inc.,
270 Madison Avenue,
New York, New York.

RBParke:jfh   1-19-45

In reply please
refer to: 79495

JAN 24, 1945

To: Mr. Norman P. Davis, Manager,
Foreign FundsControl Department.

From: E. W. O'Flaherty,
Special Assistant to the Director

There is enclosed for your information and
guidance a copy of license No. W-2402, issued under even
date, to the American Jewish Joint Distribution Committee,
Inc., 270 Madison Avenue, New York, New York, authorizing
it to remit the sum of Swiss francs 20,000,000 to a banking
institution in Switzerland for credit to a joint account in
the names of Saly Mayer, President of the Swiss Jewish
Refugee Fund and Roswell D. McClelland, Representative of
the War Refugee Board in Switzerland.

217

The funds to be remitted under this license
are intended for humanitarian purposes. Mr. Rushmore,
Foreign Accounts Section, Federal Reserve Bank of New York,
has also been furnished a copy of this license.

(Signed) E. W. O'Flaherty

RBParke:mbw 1-20-45

MEMORANDUM

For attachment to:

FFC Letter No:

Date: January 24, 1945

TO: Liaison Officer, Foreign Funds Control

FROM: War Refugee Board

Subject:

Rescue and relief in enemy territory.

There is transmitted herewith a copy of a letter dated from Miss Model
/xxxxxxxxxxx

from the   dealing with the remittance

of 20,000,000 Swiss francs by the American Jewish Joint Distribution Committee
to a banking institution in Switzerland for credit to a joint account in the
names of Saly Mayer and Roswell D. McClelland for special rescue negotiations
conducted under the supervision of Mr. McClelland.

218

The War Refugee Board recommends that appropriate Treasury
licenses and other necessary documents be issued permitting the execution
of the project contemplated in the letter described above.

Remarks:

See attached memorandum.

For the War Refugee Board

Action:

Basic license No. W-2402 issued January 25, 1945
Remittance license No.   issued
Other: Letter No. 80181 to Rushmore, NY Fed., January 25, 1945

R: B. Parks
Liaison Officer
Foreign Funds Control

Date:
January 25, 1945

Jan 25, 1945

To: Mr. Rushmore,
         Foreign Accounts Section,
         Federal Reserve Bank of New York.

From: E. W. O'Flaherty,
         Special Assistant to the Director.

There is enclosed for your information and
guidance a copy of license No. W-2402, issued under
even date, to the American Jewish Joint Distribution
Committee, Inc., 270 Madison Avenue, New York, New
York, authorizing it to remit the sum of Swiss
francs 20,000,000 to a banking institution in Switzer-
land for credit to a joint account in the names of
Saly Mayer, President of the Swiss Jewish Refugee
Fund and Roswell D. McClelland, Representative of the
War Refugee Board in Switzerland.

The funds to be remitted under this license
are intended for humanitarian purposes.

219